What is Spirituality?

What is Spirituality?

And is it for me?

PETER TOON

daybreak
London

First published in 1989 by
Daybreak
Darton, Longman and Todd Ltd
89 Lillie Road, London SW6 1UD

British Library Cataloguing in Publication Data

Toon, Peter
    What is spirituality?
    1. Christian life. Spirituality
    I. Title
    248′.4

    ISBN 0–232–51804–1

Phototypeset by Input Typesetting Ltd,
London SW19 8DR
Printed and bound in Great Britain by
Anchor Press Ltd, Tiptree, Essex

For
The Lord Barnard TD
patron of the parish of
Staindrop, County Durham

Contents

PART THREE Fulfilling Every Duty

PART FOUR Choosing the Way

Preface

Spirituality has become an 'in' word. Inside and outside the churches people are talking about it – or at least using the word. Publishers are listing a growing number of volumes under the heading 'Books on Spirituality': conferences and retreats are advertised as means of increasing spirituality: various bodily and mental disciplines are being recommended by priest and guru as ways of finding or developing spirituality: and even some psychotherapists have adopted techniques of spirituality to cure the soul.

But is spirituality something which you and I ought to get involved in? Is it really for me and is it truly for you? Maybe it is merely the latest non-materialistic fad, which, like this year's fashion, will soon be out of date; or, perhaps, it is only a fancy word for old-fashioned insights and practices which were called by other names in earlier centuries. Maybe pursuing spirituality is like chasing a runaway horse; or, perhaps, becoming too involved in it is like diving into a pool full of sharks!

'What is spirituality?' and 'Is it for me?' are two very different questions. The first requires a carefully presented, factual answer which is based upon sound knowledge of the Bible, theology and religious experience. A slick and quick answer will not do: it must ring true to our best thinking and mature experience. The second question can only be answered by you or me for ourselves. So what we need are guidelines and the means by which to answer. Deciding for or against spirituality is a moral decision. It is not like choosing a new car or coat or house: it is all about accepting or rejecting what is perceived as what God offers and demands.

Parts two and three are an answer to the question, 'What is

(Christian) spirituality?' and they follow on from chapter two of Part one. Part four provides the guidelines for answering the question, 'Is spirituality for me?' Part one prepares the way for the presentations in Parts two, three and four.

I have much enjoyed the research and reflection which have gone into the writing of this book. I hope and pray that many readers will believe that they have benefited from studying it.

Before inviting my reader to begin Part one, I feel I ought to make clear that this book is not a 'how to do it' kind of book. I shall give no *detailed* guidance on such topics as – how to read the Bible profitably; how to meditate upon its contents; how to pray effectively; how to fast and keep a shining face; how to obey Christ's commands in everyday situations; how to be a devout mother/father/son/daughter and how to find inner peace and quiet in a bustling world. There are many books on such topics: some very helpful.

Rather, I attempt to supply the reader with the basic structure which has to exist before the 'how to do it' question can be taken seriously. In other words I provide the skeleton on which the flesh can grow and I offer the structure to which all parts can be bolted.

I see this book as eminently practical. Yet it is more like the practical work of the architect than of the bricklayer and painter. We need both the architect and the craftsmen to produce a sound building: and we need both the general outline and plan of spirituality as well as the 'how to do it' help. In saying this I have to admit that thinking about the general outline and structure of spirituality is more demanding on the brain than considering practical suggestions on, for example, how to pray. However, I believe that most people will think the extra effort needed is well worth making.

Finally, I want to express my appreciation to my editor, Morag Reeve, for entrusting me with this topic, and to Canon David Wheaton, His Honour Judge Brian Watling, Dr Steve Motyer, and Vita (my wife) for reading the manuscript and offering helpful criticism.

PETER TOON
Feast of the Transfiguration
6 August 1988

PART ONE

Clarifying Basic Issues

1

Removing Half-truths

In June 1988 I had an interesting conversation by the River Thames in London with Richard Foster, author of *The Celebration of Discipline*. We discussed what sincere Christians in biblically-based congregations were looking for in terms of growth in Christ and the faith. He told me that in America he finds that many are asking such questions as: Where do I go from here [i.e. from my having made a decision for Christ]?, and how do I begin to move forward [on the narrow way that leads to eternal life]? and how do I change [so that I become more life Jesus]? Apparently there is – at least in some areas – too much emphasis on birth and too little on growth. What is needed is more teaching on growing into Christ for those who have entered the narrow door into the Christian way. You can only be born once but you must keep growing! And you need to grow in a rounded way towards maturity.

In April 1987 I had a series of interesting conversations with Simon Chan in Singapore. Dr Chan is soon to publish an important book on meditation with Cambridge University Press. We discussed what was needed in the charismatically-renewed congregations of that island. He explained to me that along with their joyous emphasis on celebration in worship he saw the need to introduce asceticism (by which he meant discipline and order and duties). For while many, baptised in the Holy Spirit, were rejoicing in the Lord they felt that they were not growing: they were living on the same diet, as it were, which kept them rejoicing as they stood still. They needed – and were asking for – help in order to grow deeper into Christ.

I hardly need add that in my home country, Britain, the

3

same interest and concern for growth and maturity is expressed by people of varying ages and traditions.

What is desired in America, Singapore and Britain is (in modern terms) a deeper spirituality. And this is the background which has already inspired me to write several books. My *Longing for the heavenly realm* (London, 1987) is about meditating upon the exalted Lord Jesus Christ in heaven in order to have his mind and know his will. My *From Mind to Heart: Christian Meditation Today* (Grand Rapids, 1987) is a general introduction (for American students) to the biblical basis and historical practice of meditating upon Christian themes. Then my *Meditating upon God's Word: Prelude to Prayer and Action* (London, 1988) is a call to practise seriously the art of meditating daily upon a part of the Bible.

Apart from writing my own books I have edited two important classics in this field of spirituality – Francis de Sales, *Introduction to the Devout Life* (London, 1988) and *Christ for all Seasons: Meditations for Lent, Easter and Christmas* by Thomas à Kempis (Basingstoke, 1989). The original title of the latter was *Orationes et Meditationes* (Prayers and Meditations). I hope it is true to say that I have learnt a lot from reading the classics of the spiritual life – be they Catholic or Protestant.

I do not claim to be an expert on spirituality or to be a saint in daily living (those who know me would confirm this statement!). However, I do seek the Lord and I am a serious and careful searcher after truth in this whole area of Christian growth and maturity. I do study, meditate and pray. And in this book I try my best to be as clear and as simple as possible in my account of spirituality.

I would say that this book is no more difficult than Richard Foster's *Celebration of Discipline* but more difficult than Joyce Huggett's *Listening to God*. This is because I attempt to analyse important ideas, concepts and themes as they appear in Scripture; and these do not lend themselves to illustration by the kind of moving personal stories that Joyce uses in her books.

However, my friends who have read this book in manuscript tell me that those who read it slowly and carefully will benefit much from its contents. I hope you will find this to be true and that you will make the effort to read and think about its teaching.

A book has to be targeted to a particular readership: one cannot write for everybody. This book is written primarily for those who would place themselves – generally speaking – in the evangelical and/or charismatic schools of thought and experience. In other words I have kept in mind those Christians who insist on the importance of personally confessing Jesus as Saviour and Lord: further, I have borne in mind their high view of the Holy Scriptures as God's Word and their belief in the dynamic presence of the Holy Spirit. To have done so is not difficult for I share these basic commitments. I fully recognise that others from different traditions share these emphases: I sincerely hope they too will benefit from my writing.

Before attempting to state precisely what is spirituality, I believe that it will be helpful to remove some misunderstandings. Here are twelve different views/definitions/descriptions of the content of spirituality which I think are unsatisfactory. Considering them will help us gain clarity of mind to be able to form a satisfactory definition of this elusive word.

1. *Spirituality means taking over or adopting certain Roman Catholic or Greek Orthodox practices and doctrines.* 'To be truly spiritual you must call the Lord's Supper the Eucharist and receive Holy Communion as often as possible; you must pray to Mary, mother of our Lord, as well as to all the saints asking for their help; you must carefully observe holy days and saints' days; you must highly value candles in church; and you must insist that clergy wear proper vestments.'

Our reply is that spirituality does not require a devout Protestant to imitate devotional practices from Roman Catholicism or Greek Orthodoxy: however, she/he may learn much about prayer from these traditions.

2. *Spirituality is adopting Eastern forms of meditation in order to get in touch with 'reality'.* 'Civilised people are not in touch with reality. They confuse the world as it truly is with the world as they think about it, talk about it and describe it. By meditation you strip off the layers of false consciousness; you

unlearn that which you have learned; and you begin to see clearly who and what you are. You come to experience the real world deep within yourself and all around you.'

Our response is that spirituality does not require a devout Protestant to adopt techniques of meditation developed in the East in Buddhism, Hinduism and Yoga: however, she/he may learn much about self-discipline from these traditions.

3. *Spirituality is gained by going off on regular retreats.* 'You are living in a busy, frenzied world. It is difficult to find space and time to be silent. To become spiritual you need to get away to a retreat centre to give God a chance to meet you, and you him. In this setting you will be fortified to live as a Christian in the daily world.'

Our comment is that spirituality does not require all Christians to go off on regular retreats. It does, however, require that 'when you pray, go into your room, close the door and pray to your Father, who is unseen' (Matt 6:6; cf Mk 6:31).

4. *Spirituality is acquired by participation in celebratory events.* 'The Lord is wonderfully present at Keswick/Spring Harvest where God's people celebrate his salvation and praise his name. You must go there to be inspired and uplifted. Your batteries will not merely be recharged: they will be both renewed and fully charged.'

Our view is that spirituality does not require all Christians to attend special, intense, and moving meetings. It does, however, require 'everything that has breath to praise the Lord' (Ps 150).

5. *Spirituality is gained by being as busy as possible for Jesus.* 'There is so much to be done for the kingdom of God. The fields are ripe for harvest. People are hungry for the gospel and you must declare it to them; people are in need of practical help and you must serve them; your church has meetings most evenings and you must support them. Only by keeping active will you grow in spiritual life as a Christian.'

We claim that busyness for Jesus is the fruit of spirituality not its cause. The genuine Christian life is a dynamic union of the active and prayerful aspects, or the active and meditative/contemplative dimensions.

6. *Spirituality is reading and discussing the latest, 'top-of-the-chart' books on the spiritual life.* 'Have you read *Celebration of Discipline* by Richard Foster [or *God of Surprises* by Gerard Hughes or *Listening to God* by Joyce Huggett]? It's really exciting and tells you how to be a real Christian today. Just get hold of it and see what it has to say. You'll be into a deeper Christian life very quickly.'

We believe that reading good books can be very helpful and inspiring. But spirituality is all about the state of the mind, heart and the will: what is read has to be put into practice.

7. *Spirituality is reading classics from the past, especially those which deal with contemplative prayer.* 'Have you read the anonymous *The Cloud of Unknowing* or *The Revelations of Divine Love* by Mother Julian? You need to discover contemplation and silence, and these and similar books are *the* way into it. For as Richard Rolle said, 'Contemplation is a wonderful joy of God's love' (in his *The Fire of Love*).'

We know that reading the classics of contemplative prayer can be helpful at the right time in the Christian pilgrimage. But spirituality involves much more than attempting to be silent and to engage in contemplative prayer.

8. *Spirituality is the search for special experiences of the gifts of the Spirit in prayer, fellowship and worship.* 'Have you ever felt a warm glow in your heart as you have begun to speak in tongues, to prophesy or to utter a word of wisdom (1 Cor 12)? God wants you not only to receive the gifts of the Spirit but also to feel their power and his love deep in your heart. The Spirit of Christ will witness with your spirit that you are a child of God and there is no greater inner experience than this.'

Our reply is that spirituality most certainly includes the reception and use of the gifts of the Spirit from the ascended Lord Jesus. However, it also involves self-discipline, mortification of the sinful self and asceticism.

9. *Spirituality is the way to true self-fulfilment and wholeness*. 'You are a unity. While modern life usually makes adequate provision for body and mind, it bypasses the spirit. If you are going to be an integrated personality God calls you as an individual to cultivate and nourish your spirit. You must learn to pray, meditate and participate in acts of worship.'

Our response is that spirituality certainly involves the individual but the individual as a member of the body of Christ, and a citizen of the heavenly Jerusalem. Further, spirituality emphasises self-fulfilment within the purposes of God in the body of Christ since you are called to enjoy God and to glorify him forever.

10. *Spirituality is only for pastors, leaders and elders in the churches*. 'You are too busy to find time for Bible-study and prayer; you find talk about doctrines and ethics too difficult; and if you become super-holy no one will understand you or even listen to you. Leave the search for spirituality to those who have time and who are our leaders.'

Our comment is that spirituality is for all. However, the methods and expressions of it will differ according to personal circumstances. God calls all to perfection and holiness but not by identical routes.

11. *Spirituality only arises from the study of the Bible which is the Word of God*. 'The Bible is the written Word of God. You must read, study and learn it. You must meditate upon it daily. For through these means the spiritual life is nurtured. There is no substitute for knowing the Word of God.'

Our view is that spirituality is certainly based on the Word; but it is also concerned with the right reception of the sacraments of Baptism and Holy Communion. Further, it is uniquely about a personal union within the body of Christ with the Lord Jesus: and we encounter him through both Word and sacraments.

12. *Spirituality only truly begins when a person is baptised in or with the Holy Spirit – or when the second blessing is received*. 'God has promised to fill us with his Spirit and until this event

occurs you are walking on the lower not the higher road of holiness. Only when you are lifted through the direct action of the Spirit of the Lord Jesus onto the higher road do you truly begin to be spiritual.'

We certainly hold that spirituality is increased by the direct action of the Spirit upon our souls. However, alongside the heavenly intervention is to go our self-discipline and commitment to travel through the narrow gate along the hard and narrow way. (Matt 7:13–14).

To bring this chapter to a close it will be useful and helpful to make ourselves aware of some of the dangers which meet us at every turn in our western society. They do not oppose spirituality as such: rather they manipulate it so that it becomes something other than what it ought to be. The best is replaced by the good; or, worse still, by the inferior and unbalanced.

Here are three very common dangers. Through reflection you will be able to expand them as well as add others. They relate to some of the false views listed above.

a. *The danger of individualism*. In western society it is generally assumed that I have rights, choices, preferences and views which must be taken into account by others. In fact, my rights must be honoured. We think of the individual first and society second (individuals making up society) rather than society first and the individual second (society composed of individuals).

Christian spirituality says with St Paul: 'I have been crucified with Christ and I no longer live, but Christ lives in me' (Gal 2:20). And also: 'In Christ you are being built together to become a dwelling in which God lives by his Spirit' (Eph 2:22). Here the 'you' is plural. The pressure of individualism pushes us towards seeing spirituality as a means of self-fulfilment and self-realisation (see 2 and 9 above).

b. *The danger of superficiality*. In today's world, by reading newspapers and magazines and watching TV, we gain a minimal, lop-sided knowledge of a wide variety of subjects. Because of the speed and mobility of society we meet many people but know very little about most of them. We have gained much in breadth but lost out on depth.

Spirituality is concerned with depth and says with St Paul: 'I consider everything a loss compared to the surpassing greatness of knowing Jesus Christ my Lord, for whose sake I have lost all things. I consider them rubbish, that I may gain Christ and be found in him . . .' (Phil 3:8–9). The pressure of superficiality causes us to count our union with Christ as only of general, not particular and unique, importance. It is one amongst several important things in life.

c. *The danger of doing or taking things up merely for their immediate advantage or usefulness*. We sometimes take a long term view of things. However, drinking instant coffee and eating ready-made TV meals we usually look for immediate results from our activity and investments. We do not save up to buy what we want: we buy it now on credit: we tend to value things in terms of their usefulness in the short term only.

The tests we apply to determine what is worthwhile are often merely pragmatic. We do not ask, for example, whether worship, prayer, contemplation and meditation are right and good for their own sakes: but we ask about the practical benefits they produce in the short term.

Spirituality is committed to the long term – to life everlasting – and says with St Paul: 'Forgetting what is behind and straining to what is ahead, I press on towards the goal to win the prize for which God has called me heavenwards in Christ Jesus' (Phil 3:14). The pressure of wanting immediate results makes us think that we can and ought to be achieving Christian maturity very quickly. When this does not occur we can become impatient, depressed and disillusioned.

Therefore, if we desire to engage in, and partake of, genuine spirituality we need to be aware of these dangers.

2

Defining Spirituality

Recently I had the pleasure – and the hard work – of editing a book entitled, *Guidebook to the Spiritual Life* (Basingstoke, 1988). Of the twenty-five contributors I chose Joyce Huggett to write the first chapter entitled, 'What is spirituality?'. Her positive answer, enriched by moving stories, was in the following terms.

She began with the statement: 'Christian spirituality starts with God. He yearns to flood the life of everyone with his own holy life and love.' And she added that the Holy Spirit creates within us 'that capacity for God without which we cannot be filled with the divine life and love because we are so full of self.' Therefore, she continued by explaining that 'it is hardly surprising that the language of . . . spirituality seems punctuated by words like desire, thirst, hunger, pining, panting, homesickness, languishing, sighing, seeking, restlessness, and yearning'.

Spirituality is the response of 'love to Love' and thus is practical in everyday situations. 'God's life is drawn from us so that we may become the channel through which his life flows out to others to bring them refreshment, cleansing, food, healing or the opportunity for growth or mere survival.'

I welcome this approach and the comment that 'spirituality is the means through which God continually tops up our own supplies and develops the landscape of our lives'. But I recognise – as you do – that many people today do not have the confidence of Joyce Huggett and are confused as to what is spirituality. So let us investigate! And let us be honest. To attempt to define spirituality is not easy: even using a pres-

11

tigious dictionary is not as helpful as we might think it ought to be.

If you turn to the *Oxford English Dictionary* (1971) and look up 'spirituality' you will find the following information. The first meaning and one much used several centuries ago, is 'the body of spiritual or ecclesiastical persons'. This refers to the clergy as a group or body, e.g. meeting in a synod.

The second meaning, and one again much used a few centuries ago, is 'that which has a spiritual character: ecclesiastical property or revenue held or received in return for spiritual services'. An example of this is the legal freehold of a parish and the tithes due to the rector, who ministers to the parish.

Passing by the third meaning we note that the fourth, fifth and sixth meanings all point to 'the fact or state of being immaterial, incorporeal and/or pure spirit'. Thus God's spirituality is his existence as eternal, pure Spirit and human spirituality refers to acts of the soul which are totally independent of the body. These usages are rare today.

THE SPHERE OF THE SPIRIT

The third meaning is much nearer to our concern in this book. It is 'the quality or condition of being spiritual: attachment to or regard for things of the spirit as opposed to material or worldly interests'. When I read the examples of usage cited beneath this definition I was quite excited. One of them was from the writings of a theologian of the seventeenth century, whose biography I have written. He is John Owen (1616–1683), a Puritan and for a time the Dean of Christ Church, Oxford.

In his book, *The Nature, Power, Deceit and Prevalency of the Remainders of Indwelling Sin in Believers* (1668), Owen wrote these words: 'The more of spirituality and holiness is in any thing, the greater is its [i.e. sin's] enmity. That which hath most of God hath most of [sin's] opposition' (chapter four). He was saying that sin becomes a real and powerful enemy in those souls which are under the influence of the gospel and the

Spirit of Christ. By spirituality he understood 'the sphere in and over which the Holy Spirit has direct influence'. This meaning is confirmed by his usage in other writings. For example in his *Several Practical Cases of Conscience Resolved* (published posthumously in 1721) he wrote that those who felt they were failing in the performance of their duties to Christ were 'to labour to bring spirituality into their duties' (fourth address). He meant that they were to be open to the grace of God, the presence and power of the Holy Spirit, in order that such duties as prayer and caring for the poor could be done in a way pleasing to God. He added: 'So that if we would bring spirituality into duty, it is to exercise the graces that are required by the rule to the performance of that duty.'

The addition of the suffix 'ity' to a word usually has the effect of causing that word to express a state or condition. Thus spirituality is the state/condition of being spiritual, that is of being indwelt and guided by the Holy Spirit. We find this meaning in a book by one of the leading English Nonconformist pastors and theologians of the eighteenth century, Philip Doddridge. In *The Rise and Progress of Religion in the Soul* (1745) he included these words as part of a prayer at the end of chapter xxvi: 'May I grow in patience and fortitude of soul, in humility and zeal, in *spirituality* and a heavenly disposition of mind and in a concern that whether present or absent I may be accepted of the Lord that whether I live or die it may be for his glory.'

Over a century later there appeared a book by Henry Drummond, the Scottish evangelist, with the title *Natural Law in the Spiritual World* (1883). It was a bestseller and in chapter four we find he writes: 'No spiritual man ever claims that his *spirituality* is his own.' Why? Because it is the result of the indwelling and influence of the Holy Spirit.

Some twenty years after the appearance of Drummond's book there appeared a *Commentary on 1 Corinthians* by the Anglican Dr H.L. Goudge, Principal of Wells Theological College. He used the word 'spirituality' in the same way as Drummond, Doddridge and Owen (and of course many more English priests, pastors and theologians). He wrote: 'But the Spirit of God can deal with a man as a whole and in the highest devotion the whole man – body, soul and spirit – is yielded to his influence. The right use of the mind no more interferes with the *spirituality* of our devotion than the right use of the body does' (p.128).

This meaning, of the sphere in which the Spirit dwells and works, has continued into the second half of the twentieth century. I had a phone call the other day from someone who asked: 'Is spirituality the same as sanctification?' I said, 'It can be!' However, as we shall soon see, it has been eclipsed by another meaning. This is perhaps to be regretted as the older meaning can rightly claim a sound basis in the New Testament.

The adjective 'spiritual' is used in the New Testament for that which is the result of the Holy Spirit's action – as in his giving, inspiring, illuminating, guiding and blessing. There are spiritual gifts (1 Cor 12:1; 14:1), truths (1 Cor 2:13, 9:11; Col 1:9), songs (Eph 5:19; Col 3:16), blessings (Eph 1:3), sacrifices (1 Pet 2:5) and baptised believers (1 Cor 2:15; 3:1; 12:1; 14:37). Thus, from this foundation, with the addition of 'ity' we gain the sphere or state or condition in which the Holy Spirit is operating as the Spirit of the Lord Jesus in the Church. There is, therefore, (on this approach) spirituality where there are spiritual gifts, truths, worship, service and spiritually-minded believers.

From a possible biblical usage we now turn to the popular usage today, which has more reference to human spirit than to Holy Spirit.

A VAGUE WORD?

The common meaning or popular definition today comes within the third category of the *Oxford English Dictionary* (1971). However, the sphere is of the human spirit, not of the Holy Spirit. So we learn that 'spirituality means a search for meaning and significance by contemplation and reflection on the totality of human experiences in relation to the whole world which is experienced, and also to the life which is lived, and may mature as that search proceeds' (*Spirituality for Today*, ed. Eric James, London 1968 p.61). Spirituality is all about the human search for identity, meaning, purpose, God, self-transcendence, mystical experience, integration and inner harmony. Thus there are spiritualities related to all religions and to many human pursuits which arise in the human spirit.

A Roman Catholic theologian offers this definition: 'In its widest sense spirituality refers to any religious or ethical value that is concretized as an attitude or spirit from which one's actions flow. This concept of spirituality is not restricted to any particular religion; it applies to any person who has a belief in the divine or transcendent and fashions a life-style according to one's religious convictions' (Jordan Aumann, *Spiritual Theology*, London 1980, p.17).

The three editors of *The Study of Spirituality* (London, 1986) who were concerned primarily (but not exclusively) with Christianity expressed themselves in their preface in these words: ' "Spirituality", we confess, is a vague word, often used with no clear meaning, or with a wide and vague significance; but we can think of no better single word to describe our subject. We are concerned with individual prayer and communion with God, both of the 'ordinary Christian' and of those with special spiritual gifts, and the outer life which supports and flows from this devotion.'

Gordon S. Wakefield, editor of the *Dictionary of Spirituality* (London, 1983), tells us that spirituality has come 'much into vogue to describe those attitudes, beliefs, practices which animate people's lives and help them to reach out towards super-sensible realities' (p.361).

What appears to have happened this century (and to have been accelerated in the last two or three decades) is that the basic understanding of spirit/Spirit is no longer controlled by the general doctrines of the Christian religion. Any activity of the human spirit is eligible for being described as spirituality. And the fact that we live in a pluralistic and secularist society gives a certain validity to this comprehensive and vague definition. This situation certainly means that if anyone is to use the word today then she/he must be clear what particular meaning is being offered or developed.

NATURAL SPIRITUALITY

Thus I must say how I understand and intend to use the word, spirituality. First of all I accept the approach of David Benner, editor of the *Encyclopedia of Psychology* (Grand Rapids, 1985). In his *Psychotherapy and the Spiritual Quest* (Grand Rapids, 1988) he makes a distinction between natural and religious spirituality, and sees Christian spirituality as a special form or type of religious spirituality.

From his own studies and research as a psychologist he offers the following definition of natural spirituality:

> Spirituality is the response to a deep and mysterious human yearning for self-transcendence and surrender. This yearning results from having been created in such a fashion that we are incomplete when we are self-encapsulated. As important as relationships with other people are, we need something more than involvement with others; something within us yearns for surrender to the service of some person or cause bigger than ourselves. When we experience this self-transcendent surrender, we suddenly realize that we have found our place. It may be that we never before recognized that our restlessness was our search for our place. However, when we find it we immediately know that this is where we belong. Again spirituality is our response to these longings. (p.104)

This definition allows for both a variety of natural and religious spirituality as well as for wholehearted commitment to absorbing causes and personalities. The need for self-transcendence and surrender can either be directed towards the living God or to one of numerous 'gods'. And what distinguishes a natural from a religious spirituality is that the latter involves a relationship with a supernatural power or being who serves as the focus of the self-transcendence and the meaning of life. Further, in Christian spirituality the probings and responses to deep spiritual longings occur within the Christian faith and fellowship of believers.

CHRISTIAN SPIRITUALITY

In the second place, I combine the general approach of Dr Benner with the particular meaning of spirituality as *response* to God which has been developed, especially by Roman Catholic writers. This meaning underlies the still incomplete *Dictionnaire de la Spiritualité* (Paris, 1932–) and the histories of spirituality by Pierre Pourrat and Louis Bouyer.

The Spanish abbot, Gabriel M. Braso, states that 'spirituality is the particular way of conceiving and of realising the ideal of the Christian life' (*Liturgy and Spirituality*, Collegeville, Minn., 1971, p.3). And Columba Cary-Elwes tells us that spirituality is all about 'the ways in which Christians at different times and in different situations have followed the guidance of the Spirit of Christ in their lives. It can be said, therefore, to be in the life and history of the Church at its deepest level' (*Experiences with God. A Dictionary of Spirituality and Prayer*, London, 1986, p.201).

So I work with the following definition of Christian spirituality. It is *the particular way (which as a baptised believer I choose) of conceiving the goal and aim of the Christian life; and, also, the particular way (I choose) of practically working and moving towards this goal and aim*. Therefore, I am thinking of the human response (guided by the Holy Spirit) to the revelation of God in Jesus Christ and his call to draw near to him as he has drawn near to me, and to do so in the fellowship of Christ's body. And because I am thinking in this way I am able to incorporate the older meaning of spirituality which we noticed in the quotations from John Owen and Philip Doddridge, but to do so in a modern setting.

That is, I believe that I come to see the goal and aim of the Christian life through the illumination of the Holy Spirit: and I rely on the guidance and power of the Holy Spirit to offer a right response to God's revelation and grace. However, it is truly my (and your) response: it is what I think, feel and do for Christ's sake. Yet there in the background, hidden from view, is the constant presence and operation of the Spirit of the Lord Jesus. Spirituality is the way in which I respond to his action upon my spirit.

LOOKING TO THE LORD

I want also to suggest that any genuine Christian spirituality will include what may be described as a fourfold look or gaze upon the Lord and his revelation. That is, the dynamic local church and true disciple will have spiritual eyes which look in four directions simultaneously. However, the gaze will not be of equal intensity in each direction.

The gaze which must be considered first, and which is the source and inspiration of the other three, is the *looking up* to God in faith through our Lord Jesus Christ. 'Let us fix our eyes on Jesus, the author and perfecter of our faith' (Heb 12:2). Faith looks to God in and through Jesus Christ in meditation, prayer and contemplation. (I have developed this theme in my *Longing for the Heavenly Realm*, Hodder and Stoughton, 1987, MacMillan USA, 1988, and I think it is far more important that much western contemporary Christian teaching appears to allow.)

To look up in faith requires that we *look back* as we read the records of God's revelation in the Old and New Testaments. We see God at work in human history. Not only do we look back we also *look forward* in hope to the seeing of God in the perfection of heaven – 'blessed are the pure in heart for they shall see God'. Finally, to look up to God in faith implies that we *look around* and see his revelation through nature and his providence in history: for God is always present in and through his creation.

We extend the *looking back* to the events and teaching recorded in Holy Scripture to include the experience of God enjoyed by the Church over the centuries. So spirituality includes both the necessary meditating upon Scripture and the (recommended) reading of spiritual classics (e.g. Augustine's *Confessions* and Bunyan's *Pilgrim's Progress*).

We expand the *looking forward* to include not only the glorious vision of and enjoyment of God in the age to come but also the second coming of Jesus Christ to close the history of this age, to raise the dead, to judge the world and to inaugurate the new order of the kingdom of God.

And we intensify the *looking around* both to see God

revealed in his creation and to see human beings, made in his image, calling for our love, respect and care. To love the neighbour is a natural outcome of gazing upon God in the face of Jesus Christ our Lord.

It is perhaps necessary to add a comment here upon the nature of the looking upon God as he is revealed in the created order and in human events. This is a positive gaze even though the world as we know it is seriously affected by sin and suffering (see further chapters three and four). The character of it has been well expressed by my former professor, Eric Mascall, in his moving book, *Grace and Glory* (1975). He asks the question: 'What is our attitude to the world to be?' And his reply is as follows:

> Treat it as if it is all there is and as if all that you need is to be found in it, and it will dangle its gifts before your eyes, decoy you, tantalize you, and finally mock and desert you, leaving you empty handed and with ashes in your mouth. But treat it as the creation of God, as truly good because it is God's handiwork and yet not the highest good because it is not God himself; live in this world as one who knows that his true home is not here but in eternity and the world itself will yield up to you its joys and splendours of whose very existence the mere worldling is utterly ignorant. Then you will see the world's transience and fragility, its finitude and its powerlessness to satisfy, not as signs that life is a bad joke with man as the helpless victim, but as pale and splintered reflections of the splendour and beauty of the eternal God in whom alone man can find lasting peace and joy.

Here natural spirituality is converted by God's grace into an important part of everyday Christian spirituality.

Before we move on in Part Two to look at the goal/aim of the Christian life and in Parts Three and Four at the ways and means of reaching the goal and fulfilling the aim, we need to set the general context in which we can appreciate the nature of Christian spirituality. Therefore, in the rest of Part One we shall examine the possibility for spirituality in the make-up of human beings as creatures made by the Lord God to have communion with him and to serve him everlastingly.

3

In the Image of God

In the first chapter of the Bible the special status of human beings in God's creation is expressed by God himself in these words: 'Let us make man in our own image, in our likeness' (Gen 1:26). The words 'image' and 'likeness' reinforce each other for (in the Hebrew) there is no 'and' between them.

IN GOD'S LIKENESS

As a living creature who thinks, feels and acts in and through a physical body, the human person is made in the image, after the likeness of the Creator of the universe. Thus men and women are not only 'above the animals' because they are thinking and moral beings; they also possess a relationship (or at least the possibility of one) with God. This begins in this mortal life and can last everlastingly into the age to come. We are like God because we are spiritual beings. We have a God-given capacity to have fellowship with the eternal Spirit, through our human spirits.

Further, as unique creatures in God's creation, we have a special duty to be stewards and priests of this created order. What this means is well brought out by the rabbinic story based on Genesis 1. It goes like this.

At the end of the fifth day of creation God surveyed the universe he had made out of nothing and was well pleased with what he saw of its shape and living contents. So the Creator asked one of his attendant archangels whether there was anything missing. In reply the archangel first complimented God on his marvellous creation which was so grand and beautiful

21

and perfect. Then he suggested, with some hesitation, that perhaps there was one thing missing. 'And what is that?' asked the Lord God. 'It is speech to make what is already perfect more perfect; speech to praise its perfection' came the reply.

'What a wonderful idea', God responded. Then he went ahead and made the human creature, intending that in him the whole creation should find, and be expressed through, a voice; and that in him the whole inarticulate creation should become articulate. The speaking God intended that he should be heard by and replied to by a speaking animal.

So human beings only are truly fulfilled as they both enjoy communion with their God and as they praise him on behalf of all his creatures. We have been made both to respond to our Creator and to serve him as his stewards in the created order. We have been given the capacity to hear what he says, feel his presence, power and glory and to address him in prayer and praise. And we have been called to imitate him in all his ways.

David, the shepherd, is the writer of Psalm 8. We can picture him sleeping out in the fields and looking up to the sky before composing this moving poem. It includes these lines:

> When I consider your heavens,
>   the work of your fingers,
> the moon and the stars,
>   which you have set in place
> what is man that you are mindful of him
>   the son of man that you care for him?
> You made him a little lower than the heavenly beings
>   and crowned him with glory and honour.

Living as we do in the days of advanced cosmology and astrophysics, we know far more than David did about the vastness of the universe. As we contemplate it we must also say, 'What is the human being?' He/she is so tiny, so fragile, and so frail, set in such a massive universe with so many galaxies.

Yet, while it is true that the human being – you or I – is so little and insignificant in comparison with the totality of God's creation, it is also true that, from the perspective of the Creator, the human being is actually great. 'You have made him a little lower than the heavenly beings (archangels and angels) and crowned him with glory and honour.' If you compare the human being with the whole creation then she/he shrinks into nothingness. If you compare the human being with her/his Creator then a marvellous thing occurs: instead of becoming more insignificant she/he becomes special – in fact unique. This is because the human being is made in the image of God, after his likeness. Psalm 8 is at least in part a meditation upon Genesis 1.

The human animal has been given rational powers – she/he is an original thinker and can look at herself/himself and make an evaluation. Also the human animal has a moral sense, a knowledge of right and wrong, as well as an artistic gift, a sense of beauty and creativity. Then she/he has a capacity and a need to love and be loved. Therefore the human being is capable of rising to great heights of intellectual discovery, heroism and care for others. All this and more is what it means to be made in the image of God.

Regrettably, as we shall note in the next chapter, the human being is also capable of great selfishness and cruelty, of inventing hydrogen bombs and using them, of building concentration camps and filling them with defenceless people. This is because the image of God is defaced, diseased and distorted. The human being who is made a little lower than the angels in heaven is in need of salvation from sin and reconciliation with his/her Creator and Judge (see further Chapter 4 on 'inner cleansing').

Christians confess and celebrate the fact that Jesus of Nazareth did think, will and do all that being in the image, after the likeness of God requires. He lived in perfect communion with God and nothing marred this harmonious relationship. Thus he is described as being the true image of God by the apostle Paul (2 Cor 4:4; Col 1:15).

INNER YEARNING

All human creatures are made to live fruitfully in the physical and relate harmoniously to the spiritual realm. The fact of what we call sin has not removed but has distorted or diseased the image of God upon our souls. There is within all of us a yearning to be at one with creation and our Creator. This yearning is felt more strongly by some people than others.

The universality of religion and religious spirituality testifies to this inner desire to be in a right relationship with God and his world. Wherever you go in the world from Peking to Hawaii and from Leningrad to Capetown you find that people have been, and often still are, consciously religious and very much aware of the spiritual realm. Of course, there are many different descriptions of the spiritual realm/God and a great variety of rituals/practices to gain and maintain communion with the divine. Yet the fact remains that a large part of the population of the world still searches for communion with deity through traditional religious worship and ascetic practices. Tourists from the developed world often find this surprising – especially when they see the holy men of the Indian sub-continent and their apparently excessive devotion to self-denial in order to find, and be at one with, the spiritual realm.

The apparent lack of sustained religious practices and ascetic life-styles among the affluent and in the westernised part of the world does not mean that the image of God has been totally lost in these people. The yearning for God (often very weak because of the mighty pressure of secularism) expresses itself however weakly in a variety of ways. For example, at one extreme there is the great interest in adaptions of traditional Eastern yoga, meditating and dieting in order to gain inner harmony, reduce the blood pressure, sleep better and live more humanly. At the other is the growth of fundamentalism of various kinds and its appeal to people as a 'simple' way of relating to the world in all its complexity and to deity in all his demands. And in-between there is the movement which attempts to find harmony by 'communing with nature' be it through nudist colonies, camping, rambling, bird-watching or other pursuits in the outdoors. To this we must add a host of other pursuits through and by which people seek to make sense of their inner desire and yearning to affirm the spiritual as well as the material aspects of existence.

If you were to question people on the streets of London or New York as to whether or not they feel a longing for God you would probably find that the majority who replied would answer in the negative. Yet, if pressed, they would surely confess to having certain quests which originate deep within their inner selves – as polls taken by newspapers continually illustrate.

Here are a few such quests. There is the quest for *identity* (Who am I? Where do I fit in? What do I believe and what are my values?); for *happiness* (Where and when shall I find fullness of life and of personhood?); for *success* (How shall I get status, quality of life and be all I can be?); for *beauty* (Where is the art, music, dance or other area of human creativity in which I can be deeply moved and satisfied?); and for *stimulation* (How can I be fully alive and experience all there is to be experienced?).

Because we are made in the image of God, after his likeness, there is a yearning for God in all these and similar quests. The quest for identity is a search for membership of the family of God, to be a brother of the Lord Jesus; the quest for happiness is a search for the life of trust, love and obedience, whose direct fruit is happiness; the quest for success is a search to be fulfilled in doing the will of God; the quest for beauty is a search for a sight of the glory of God in the face of Jesus Christ; and the quest for stimulation is the search for being filled with the Holy Spirit.

The quest for identity, happiness, success, beauty, stimulation (and we may add for truth and justice) is, at best, a natural spirituality unless the quest is transformed by the Holy Spirit into a Christian quest and spirituality. And, let us freely admit, much of what may be called natural spirituality is good and wholesome. The inspiration, insight and illumination claimed by the painter and poet, artist and musician, writer and sculptor, craftsman and theoretical physicist, visionary and pure mathematician, are to be attributed to the Holy Spirit acting upon human spirit. But this action is as the creator Spirit, in the way of nature, not of grace.

The Holy Spirit acting in the way of grace is when he is acting as the Paraclete of Jesus (John 14:15) coming in his name in order to continue and complete his work on earth. He comes upon the human spirit and into the human soul so that we become alive to God's call and word, power and presence, in order that our natural striving and questing might be purified and given new direction and power. In other words, as the Spirit of grace, he comes to recreate the soul in the image, after the likeness of God, according to the pattern revealed in Jesus.

INNER SEARCHING

From the psychological perspective we may point to what may be described as the deep and mysterious longing/yearning for self-transcendence and surrender in human souls. This can be interpreted as an unconscious searching for our 'roots' as human creatures. That is, we have forgotten who we really are and to where we actually belong. However, we seem to have a vague memory of the original place where we belong and the original model which we are to imitate; and the place/model seems to be something other than self – a reality transcendent to self. Further, we feel that we ought to be (and need to be) in the service of a cause greater than ourselves. This searching for self-transcendence and surrender to that which is higher than ourselves constantly occurs – even when we do not wish it to do so – because we are still creatures made in God's image, in his likeness.

Connected with this searching/longing/yearning for that which is 'above' our normal experience, are the further and related quests for the integration of our being and the discovery of our true selves. We seek vital harmony and the bringing together of our internal and external lives, our thoughts and actions, and our soul and body – not to mention our thoughts and feelings, unconscious and conscious minds, and our self and ego. And as long as we seek this integration within ourselves we seem never finally to succeed or be satisfied; for we need a self-transcendent reference point outside or bigger than ourselves in order to find both the true self and integration of the self.

This search for self-discovery can easily become or be turned into a quest for self-satisfaction and self-fulfilment. And much of what in these days is called spirituality is in fact a kind of psychological spirituality which supplies a temporary form of inner harmony and fulfilment. Only when this 'natural' spirituality is guided towards the living God, who is transcendent yet always present to help, can it reach its goal and be truly satisfied. For to discover our true self, we must first die to our old self, that is to our ego. Dying to this idolatrous self-as-God we then discover the identity of our true self, our self-in-God. Christians believe that this process is only truly possible through Jesus Christ in the power of the Holy Spirit.

So religious spirituality is to be distinguished from natural or psychological spirituality. But the religion in question need not be Christianity. It can be Judaism or Islam, for example. Religious spirituality involves the cultivation of a relationship with a divine Spirit/Power/Being through meditation, prayer and discipline. And we see what may be called a religious spirituality being advocated by a lot of the modern self-help groups in society (especially in the USA). Such a group as Alcoholics Anonymous encourages those seeking release from the bondage of slavery to the demon of alcohol to pray to the Higher Power and seek a positive relationship with this Power/God/deity. It is said that it does not matter what you call the transcendent Reality/Being but to help yourself you must develop a relationship with it/him/her.

A final comment concerning the psychological perspective is necessary. It appears that people are most open to feeling and responding to the search for self-transcendence and the integration of being when they pass through a time of crisis or transition. This may be adolescence, the break-up of a love-affair or marriage, the loss of a job, the death of a loved one or movement from one place/culture to another. Of course the spiritual movement is not necessarily towards the God and Father of our Lord Jesus Christ: so much depends on what influences come to bear upon the person when in the period of crisis or transition.

4

Through, with and in Jesus

Jesus taught that God acts both invisibly and graciously as life-giving power. To the woman of Samaria with whom he talked by the well he said: 'God is spirit, and his worshippers must worship in spirit and in truth' (John 4:24). It is doubtful whether Jesus intended this as a definition of God's being: rather it is a metaphor of God's mode of action – just as 'God is light' is a metaphor of his radiant purity. God is the source of all life, yet to the human eye he is invisible, to the human ear he is silent and by the human hands he is untouchable.

We use 'spirit' of the invisible point of contact in our inner selves with our Creator and Saviour who is eternal Being. We also use the word 'soul' of our inner selves: my soul is my inner life and activity of thinking, feeling, deciding, determining and desiring. It includes the heart, mind and will. So to say with the Virgin Mary, 'My soul praises the Lord' (Luke 1:46) or with the psalmist, 'Praise the Lord, O my soul', is to glorify God with intellect, desires, feelings and intentions. Not that these aspects of the soul can be separated for we are unified creatures and the one self is active in thinking, feeling, desiring and deciding. And not that there is a separate part of the soul which is called spirit. The openness of the soul to God is spirit.

Therefore spirituality is very much the activity of the whole soul. Here, in openness to God, ideas as to what is the goal and aim of the Christian life are formed; here desire grows to reach for that goal and here intentions arise which result in actions to do the will of God. And the secret activity of God here is aimed at restoring his own image and likeness which has been defaced and marred by sin. To do this God requires

29

the willing cooperation of the forgiven sinner as he seeks fellowship with his Saviour.

INNER CLEANSING

We must stop now in our tracks and take a look at the moral and spiritual condition of human beings – the state of our own souls. The word 'sin' has been used several times in Part One. It describes (a) the state of impurity and imperfection of the human soul, and (b) the fact of human rebellion against the will of God, with the tendency to find fulfilment in selfish, rather than unselfish, acts and ends.

One thing is clear: human beings are not either as a whole or as individuals behaving as if they were created in the image of God, after his likeness. We ought to mirror God's character but we don't. Instead of reflecting love, joy, peace, justice, righteousness and mercy all of the time, we often reflect selfishness, pride, discord, bitterness, tension, injustice and disorder. Even the noblest of our race – in their honest moments – know that they fall short of the standard to which we all ought to rise.

Instead of caring for the created order on behalf of its Creator as stewards, we have been notorious in misusing, maltreating and disordering natural resources and habitats. Instead of offering the praise of the whole creation to its Creator we have thought of ourselves as self-sufficient and worthy of self-congratulation.

In other words we are sinners, living in a sinful world. Now sin is a theological word and refers both to offences against the Lord directly and indirectly (through maltreatment of his creation, animate and inanimate). If we were not sinners then we would be at peace within ourselves, with each other and with the created order of nature.

We would also find constant joy and fulfilment in doing the will of the Lord in and for his world.

However, most of us are happy for part, even much, of the time, and only a few of us are permanently unhappy. The world is not in total disarray: the creation is not wholly polluted and human beings are not entirely selfish and unjust. Indeed there is a lot of down-to-earth goodness around much of the time. This is because, despite the disease of the soul we call sin, we remain, in some degree, creatures made in the image of God, after his likeness.

What sin does – amongst other things – is to cause the human spirit to cease to be totally open to the eternal Being (the Lord) and to cause the soul to function not to the glory of God and the true good of humanity but to the promotion of self-fulfilment. So we find that, while we possess a God-given capacity for communion with our Creator and Father, we are unable rightly to exercise or use it: and while we are designed to love God with the whole of our beings and our neighbours as ourselves we cannot rise to this level of love, since we have too much self-love.

So what each of us does – as God's creatures, accountable to him as our Maker and Judge – is to build up in his accounts a great mountain of debt. We accumulate this moral debt (sin) through our failure to pay our way – that is to live as God requires us to live and to do what he commands us to do. We add to this debt every day that we live and have no hopes whatsoever (out of our own resources) of settling it or paying it off.

Thus all human beings stand before their Creator and their Judge as debtors. But we also stand before him in need of inner cleansing and spiritual renewal. The pollution and stain of sin upon spirit and soul needs to be washed away: the spirit needs a breath of new life and the soul's powers (faculties) need to be morally and spiritually renewed.

There are no exceptions to this state of affairs. The kindliest of human beings is a debtor in God's accounts: and the most charming of human beings is in need of inner cleansing by the Holy Spirit.

This is the reason why in the Old Testament there is so great an emphasis upon the right administration and participation in the sacrificial system of the Temple: for that was God's way of dealing with the problem of moral debt and spiritual pollution. And this is why in the New Testament there is so great an emphasis upon the death of Jesus as an expiation and atonement for sin. Only by death of the sinless, incarnate Son of God could our debts be cancelled by God the Father and our sins cleansed and forgiven.

While spirituality leaves to systematic theology the full exposition of the saving, atoning, reconciling work of Jesus, the Redeemer, it cannot neglect to take seriously the need for the confession of sin, repentance, forgiveness and power to overcome sin and temptation. For spirituality is for the imperfect, unclean, impure, and unworthy in order to direct them towards the perfect, the clean, the pure, and the worthy.

Nowhere is this given clearer expression than in Psalm 51, composed originally by David, but much used in Christian prayer and worship since apostolic times. The prayer (psalm) begins:

> Have mercy on me, O God,
>   according to your unfailing love;
> according to your great compassion
>   blot out my transgressions.
> Wash away all my iniquity
>   and cleanse me from my sin. (vv 1–2)

and continues:

> Create in me a pure heart, O God,
>   and renew a steadfast spirit within me.
> Do not cast me from your presence
>   or take your Holy Spirit from me.
> Restore to me the joy of your salvation
>   and grant me a willing spirit, to sustain me.
> Then I will teach transgressors your ways,
>   and sinners will turn back to you. (vv 10–13)

In this prayer we find the following ingredients of true Jewish and (as interpreted through Christ) true Christian spirituality.

There is a desire for a vital, spiritual relationship with God our Saviour, for inner cleansing and wholeness, for a pure heart (mind, imagination, feelings and will), for the presence of the Holy Spirit, for inner joy, for readiness to do God's will by a willing spirit, and a determination to serve God by making known his mercy and ways to others. In fact the whole psalm deserves our closest study and meditation before we pray it as our prayer.

CENTRED ON JESUS

What makes Christian spirituality distinctive is not that it is Christians cultivating their inner lives. Christian spirituality is unique besause it is through, with, and *in* the Lord Jesus. A brief explanation is necessary, for all three prepositions are important.

Through. As sinners we come to God for forgiveness, accept-ance, justification and eternal life through Jesus. As the Son of God made Man he is the one and only Mediator between God and his creatures. As the Lamb of God who offered himself as a pure sacrifice to expiate the sins of the world, he has taken away the barriers which prevent true fellowship between God and mankind. By his atoning death and glorious resurrection he has opened a new and living way out of sin into the presence of the Father.

We respond to God's call in the gospel and we come to him through Jesus: and this means coming to the Father not only forgiven and cleansed but also robed in the righteousness of Christ. For Jesus died for our sins and rose again for our justification. This is why traditional Christian prayer has often ended with the important words 'through Jesus Christ our Lord'. We approach our Father and are heard through Jesus and for the sake of Jesus.

With. The first disciples of Jesus lived with him, physically following him in order to learn by his example and teaching. Our discipleship is also with him for he said, 'I am with you always, to the end of the age' (Matt 28:20). We obey his word and walk/travel with him because he is with us by the presence of the Holy Spirit (who is his Paraclete and Representative – John 14:25–26; 15:26–27). We walk with him in meditation, prayer and worship and into testing/temptation, ministry (service), opposition and suffering. We know that he has not only gone before us as the Way but that he is with us now in and on that very way. And being with us he brings us comfort and strength, hope and love, faith and fortitude.

In. When we come to the Father through Jesus, the Mediator, the Father accepts us and sees us in him, enclosed within his perfected human nature. This teaching is central to the theology of Paul for whom a favourite expression is 'in Christ' (Greek – *en Christō*). A simple and rewarding task is to count how many times the expression 'in Christ' (or 'in him') occurs in Ephesians 1. Here are a few of his statements:

> Count yourselves dead to sin but alive to God *in* Christ Jesus. (Rom 6:11)

> Therefore there is now no condemnation for those who are *in* Christ Jesus. (Rom 8:1)

> Praise be to god the Father of our Lord Jesus Christ, who has blessed us in the heavenly realms with every spiritual blessing *in* Christ. (Eph 1:3)

> So then, just as you received Jesus Christ as Lord, continue to live *in* him, rooted and built up *in* him. (Col 2:6)

Since the Son of God took our flesh and nature we are united to him (through the Holy Spirit's action and by our faith) in his life, death and exaltation. We are enclosed within his 'body' and God the Father lavishes his grace upon us because he sees us in his beloved Son. Paul urges that this knowledge of God's glorious grace ought to cause all believers to think, speak and act as Christ himself did.

The inclusion of believers within the Lord Jesus is also a major theme of the Gospel of John. 'I am the vine; you are the branches. If a man remains in me and I in him, he will bear much fruit' (15:5). While the words of Jesus point to the responsibility of the disciple to remain within the vine, those of Paul emphasise the complementary truth that God has placed us by his grace in the Lord Jesus.

To summarise. Christian spirituality is centred on Jesus, the Christ, who is the same yesterday, today and forever (Heb 13:8). He is the Goal at whom we aim, the Beauty we desire, the Ideal we imitate, the Lord we obey, the Way in whom we walk, the Teacher we follow, the Truth we believe and the Life we receive. Thus the more we know of Jesus the deeper ought to be our commitment to him.

TRINITARIAN IN STRUCTURE

Certainly what makes Christian spirituality unique is that it is through, with and in Jesus, the Christ. But rightly to appreciate the centrality of Christ, Christian spirituality must exist as a response to God, the Lord, who is Father, Son and Holy Spirit.

The name which the God of Abraham, Isaac and Jacob revealed as his own to Moses was 'I am who I am' (=the Lord, Yahweh or Jehovah): and the name which Yahweh, the Lord, further revealed as the inner content of his name was 'Father, Son and Holy Spirit' (see Ex 3:14 and Matt 28:19). The Godhead is One – the Lord our God is one Lord – but exists as Three Persons or Modes of Being.

As believers we are chosen by the Father, redeemed by the Son and indwelt/sanctified by the Holy Spirit. We pray to the Father, through/with/in the Son, by the inspiration of the Holy Spirit. We follow Jesus, Incarnate Son in trusting and obeying the Father in the guidance and strength of the Holy Spirit. Our communion is with the Father and the Son by the presence and power of the Holy Spirit.

We need to think, meditate and pray trinitarianly: the doctrine of God, the Lord, as Holy Trinity, ought to be firmly embedded in our minds as the very structure through which our Christianity originates and operates. Only in this way shall we rightly interpret and understand the inner meaning of Holy Scripture, preserve our spirituality from excess, imbalance and distortion, keep ourselves from falling into error and heresy, and truly honour and glorify God, our Lord.

Within this understanding of God – three Persons in one Godhead – in mind and heart, we shall then truly respond to the Lord, through, with and in Jesus (who is Incarnate Son).

In fact true religion or true spirituality is like breathing in and breathing out. We have to breathe in before we can breathe out and our life is dependent upon our breathing. We have no energy without breathing and if we stop then we die. Before we can live as Christians – loving God and our neighbour – we have to breathe into our souls the word, love and power of God. We breathe in by faith and trust: we breathe out in love and compassion. If we do not breathe in then we cannot breathe out: without faith and trust there can be no love and compassion.

PART TWO

Aiming for the Highest

5

Be Wise

Writing in 1745 Philip Doddridge expressed this conviction: 'I am persuaded that much of the credibility and comfort of Christianity is lost, in consequence of its professors fixing their aim too low and not conceiving of their high and holy calling in so elevated and sublime a view as the nature of the Christian religion would require, and the Word of God would direct' (*The Rise and Progress of Religion in the Soul*, chap. xx). In 1738 the two brothers Charles and John Wesley had overwhelming experiences of the grace of God in Jesus Christ and they began their apostolic labours to spread scriptural holiness throughout the land of England. One of the characteristics of the Christianity of the early Methodist societies was that they aimed high, believing that God called them to be the best for him that they could possibly be.

Regrettably Christian believers all too often choose to aim low: they accommodate Christianity to what is achievable by minimum effort and commitment. It seems that only in times of spiritual renewal or revival do large numbers of Christians actually feel the interior call to aim for the highest – to be stretched in mind, heart and will in the loving and serving of God. Christian spirituality is all about aiming high and being practically committed to fulfilling that aim.

A GOAL AND IDEAL

Wisdom teaches that success in any department of life usually requires both having high standards/ideals/goals and being wholeheartedly committed to them. Without a goal at which to aim activity can be pointless. Consider the following examples.

The pilgrim always has the holy place in mind on the rough journey. The long-lost son earnestly desires the moment when he will be re-united with his mother/father. The mountaineer looks and keeps looking to the summit of the mountain, and uses all his skill to get there. The lone sailor keeps in mind the shore to which he sails, and uses all his navigational and marine skills to get there. The athlete trains regularly in order not only to take part in the race but to win it.

Christians have a *Goal*: believers are motivated by an *Aim*; the forgiven people of God are impelled by a *Vision* and an *Ideal*. That vision, ideal, aim and goal is nothing less than perfect, holy and loving union with the Lord God, who is the Father, Son and Holy Spirit. They follow Jesus who, for the joy that was set before him, gladly endured the shame and suffering of Calvary. The Lord Jesus is the *Forerunner* (Greek *prodromos*: the scout, the advance guard, the One who goes first to make it safe for others to follow – Heb 6:20). So they keep their eyes upon him, looking always to him for he is the *Pioneer* (Greek, *archēgos*), a person of pre-eminence who blazes a trail for others to follow and acts thus as Guide, Leader and Pioneer – Heb 12:2).

The Psalmist, living in the Old Covenant, could only look forward to the coming of the Messiah; but, nevertheless, his heart longed for close fellowship with his God. So we have the memorable lines:

> As the deer pants for streams of water,
>   so my soul pants for you, O God.
> My soul thirsts for God, for the living God.
>   When can I go and meet with God? (Ps 42:1–2)

As one who had been encountered and commissioned by the risen, ascended Messiah, Paul cried out:

> I consider everything a loss compared to the surpassing great-ness of knowing Christ Jesus my Lord, for whose sake I have lost all things. I consider them rubbish, that I may gain Christ

and be found in him, not having a righteousness of my own that comes from the law, but that which is through faith in Christ – righteousness that comes from God and is by faith. I want to know Christ and the power of his resurrection and the fellowship of his sufferings, becoming like him at his death, and so, somehow, to attain to the resurrection from the dead. (Phil. 3:8–11)

In other places, Paul speaks of his hope for the redemption of the body, the granting by God of a body like unto the glorious resurrection body of Christ (Rom 8:18ff; cf 1 Cor 15:35ff) in which free of sin we shall truly enjoy dynamic, loving fellowship with God-in-Christ.

The Goal and Ideal operate both as that at which we aim today and that at which we aim always. Here the work of the sculptor, painter and composer will help to illustrate the point. Only the sculptor knows what will emerge out of the piece of rock at which he chisels. He knows what he has to do: it is clearly there in his mind's eye; and the work of each day is a step towards that perfection, and can be, indeed ought to be, a perfect step. Much the same applies to the work of the painter: he sees clearly that which will be the final result of his work and each hour of painstaking labour is a part of the whole and can be, and ought to be, perfect in itself. Then take the work of the composer of a symphony or even of a short melody. Each bar can be, and ought to be, perfect as he writes it down but ever in his mind is the completed whole, the music which is constantly being heard in his inward ear. The sculptor, the painter and the composer find joy in their vision of what will be the result of their labours; and they find joy in the hard work – perhaps even suffering – of their labours day by day or hour by hour.

Jesus himself enjoyed a perfect fellowship with his heavenly Father throughout his ministry (as the Gospel of John makes abundantly clear). Yet, even that perfect daily fellowship, was not the final perfection: for he looked forward to, desired, and prayed for that greater fellowship and glory that he knew was before him through the path of Calvary and resurrection from the dead (John 17:1,5,24: Heb 12:2). Believers in Jesus, who

look to him as their Forerunner, Pioneer, Lord, and Guide,
are likewise called to both a daily and a future communion
with God (Matt 8:11; Luke 22:29–30).

As John put it: 'God is love. Whoever lives in love lives in
God, and God in him. Love is made complete among us so
that we will have confidence on the day of judgment, because
in this world we are like him. There is no fear in love. But
perfect love drives out fear, because fear has to do with punishment. The man who fears is not made perfect in love' (1 Jn
4:16–18).

Paul prayed: 'May God himself, the God of peace, sanctify
you through and through. May your whole spirit, soul and body
be kept blameless at the coming of our Lord Jesus Christ.
The One who calls you is faithful and he will do it' (1 Thess
5:23–24).

Finally to quote John again: 'Our fellowship is with the
Father and with his Son, Jesus Christ' and therefore 'we walk
in the light to the light' (1 Jn 1:3 and 7).

BOTH TODAY AND TOMORROW

Over the centuries Christians have felt the call of God to follow
Christ towards the Goal – the redemption of their bodies in
the new order of the kingdom of God. And they have expressed
this cause in various ways. Some have heard God saying, 'Be
perfect . . .'; others have heard the divine voice saying, 'Be
holy . . .' and yet others have heard the heavenly call to 'Be
righteous..' and to 'Be godly . . .' Many ordinary people have
heard the call in terms of 'Be like Jesus . . .' and 'Be victorious
for Jesus' sake . . .'

Whatever the dominant motif/model used as the basis of an
individual's thinking/desiring/longing there has been a general
agreement in all sections of the Church that in its full and
ultimate realisation the ideal belongs to the new age of the
kingdom of God. Only when our hearts, minds and wills are
totally renewed by the Spirit and cleansed from all stain of sin;
and only when we are clothed in our new resurrection bodies
and have our place in the company of the redeemed, who

worship and serve God unceasingly for Christ's sake, shall we be truly and really perfect, holy, righteous, godly and victorious. But even the perfection and holiness of heaven will be one that admits the growth from glory unto glory.

At the end of his *City of God* Augustine put the matter in these words: 'There [in heaven] we shall rest and we shall see; we shall see and we shall love; we shall love and we shall praise. Behold what shall be in the end and shall not end.' In the perfection of soul and body we shall see God through Jesus our Lord; as we see him we shall love him with all our being; and as we love him we shall praise him everlastingly. What begins in glory will grow into a richer perfection, holiness, love and praise.

However, the Ideal has always been felt to be realisable in some sense here and now in the practical realities of this sinful world and evil age. The call of God in the gospel has been, and still is, felt to be not only to a future Goal but also to strive for the Ideal now. Put in theological terms, the Goal/Ideal is both eschatological (belonging to the *eschaton*, that which shall be after the Second Coming of the Lord Jesus) and a moral imperative ('today I ought to be perfect, holy, righteous and godly').

Certainly there have been discussions and debates as to the best way of stating both the Ideal/Goal and that which is truly attainable and possible here on earth day by day. Many exaggerated claims have been made and much imprecise language has been used – usually in sincerity. Yet despite knowledge of mistakes and failures Christians continually feel the urgent call as from God to aim for the highest and to be what God wants them to be. And being in and with the Lord Jesus, they know that they are on the winning side. They claim victory in the name of Jesus.

BE VICTORIOUS

There is a long tradition in the Church expressed both in prose and poetry which portrays the Christian community as the army of Christ, soldiers involved in warfare against deadly foes. This is based on a firm foundation in the New Testament. Not only is Jesus presented in the Gospels as contending with, and finally overcoming, Satan. (Mk 1:13; Jn 13:27; 16:11), but also the Christian life is portrayed in the Epistles as involving warfare against both Satan and sinfulness (Eph 6:10ff).

There is a struggle to resist temptation, to reject sinful desires (1 Pet 2:11; Jas 4:1–2), to stay on the narrow way (Lk 13:24), to pray effectually for others and for the progress of the gospel in the Church and world (1 Cor 9:24–27; Rom 15:30; Col 2:1f; 4:12). In fact Paul urges his readers to put on the armour of light (Rom 13:12) and take the weapons of righteousness in both left and right hands (2 Cor 6:7). And he explains that 'though we live in the world we do not wage war as the world does. The weapons we fight with are not the weapons of this world. On the contrary, they have divine power to demolish strongholds' (2 Cor 10:3–5). Then in Ephesians 6 he describes these weapons and the nature of the battle against Satanic power.

This warfare is on behalf of Christ and the gospel but it serves also, in the wise providence of God, to be a means of personal growth towards perfection, holiness and righteousness. All warfare brings suffering: Jesus did not achieve the victory of his resurrection without the anguish and pain of Calvary. Victory is to share in the victory of Christ and warfare is to share in his suffering. Thus the victory available daily to the Christian as an essential part of any genuine spirituality is the victory of grace and faith (1 Jn 5:4); and finally it is the victory of the resurrection of the body in the fulness of the kingdom of God (1 Cor 15:54–57). We must bear this call to be victorious in mind as we examine perfection, holiness, righteousness and godliness.

REMOVING OBJECTIONS

Before moving on to explain the call to perfection, we must face two objections. The first is that the aim of perfection, holiness and righteousness can be judged to be selfish: it can be merely the pursuit of self-fulfilment and self-transcendence:

and it can only be an expression of personal survival and salvation.

However, if we look closely into what the call to perfection, holiness and righteousness implies and requires we shall find that it is dynamically the equivalent of the pure worship, contemplation and adoration of God. Perfection is the perfect loving of God: holiness is the seeing of God with a pure heart, and righteousness is being in a right relationship with God through Jesus, the Mediator. In fact it is being perfect, holy and righteous for Christ's sake. Thus while a profound self-fulfilment and self-transcendence is achieved it is done so through, with and in Jesus Christ, because we are made in the image, after the likeness of God himself.

The second objection is often heard these days. It goes like this: surely the ideal of service is more urgently needed in our unhappy and unequal world than the ideal of personal perfection: surely the realisation and extension of the kingdom of God is more important than the ideal of holiness: and surely worship, contemplation and adoration ought to be a means to an end – the serving of people in need. Many today seem to insist that the pursuit of peace and justice is the first duty of the Church and that meditation, prayer, worship and contemplation are to be infused with this practical theme.

The answer to this objection does not include the downgrading of serving the needy and deprived or the neglect of evangelising the non-Christian world. Rather it ensures that serving and evangelising proceed from and with the right motivation. For only when serving others flows from the pure worship and contemplation of the living God will it be a serving with humility.

Gazing upon God in the face of Jesus Christ we praise and adore him: we find nothing in ourselves that is praiseworthy and we recognise that we depend wholly on his mercy and grace. Thus we go forth from contemplating his glory and compassion relieved of our desires for self-assertion, self-justification and to be patronising. We are, therefore, prepared to serve the neighbour in humility and in the love of Jesus. Worship in spirit and in truth and the contemplating of the God of all glory and grace are the only guaranteed basis of unselfish, humble service. Where service is made the Ideal with worship being a means to that end, the great spiritual danger is of patronising people rather than humbly serving them. Jesus constantly engaged in humble service because his priority in life was communion with the Father in heaven.

So the Ideal/Goal of perfection, holiness and righteousness in terms of worship, contemplation and adoration of the Lord God is the divine way into that form and type of service and ministry which is exemplified in Jesus.

6

Be Perfect

To be perfect is the state or condition of being completed or finished without any defect or excess. Yet the perfection of the red rose in bloom is a different perfection to that of a hand-carved chair; and the perfection of the mathematical formula is a different perfection to that of the four-leaf clover.

And obviously, the perfection of God himself is a different perfection to that attainable by his creation. If God possesses absolute perfection as the eternal and infinite Lord, then the perfection reached by human beings (made in his image, after his likeness) must be a relative perfection.

Therefore, in talking about Christian Perfection – which has been the title of many books and sermons over the centuries – we are talking about relative perfection. As the Lord is holy love in his eternal and infinite Being, so we are to be filled with that holy love in our souls to the fullest extent human creatures are capable of being filled.

And, we must remember that our capability of being filled will be extended in the age to come when, free of mortal bodies, we are living in immortal, glorious bodies and, free from the stain and pull of sin, we are living in the presence of God himself.

We need to bear these distinctions in mind as we reflect upon the call of God to be perfect. We must not be either tempted to diminish it or to extend this attainable perfection of the human creature.

JESUS'S CALL TO PERFECTION

Only twice does Jesus use the word *perfect* (Gk *teleios*) with reference to the life to which God calls believers. To examine these will give us insight into what is intended by this call.

a. *If you want to be perfect, go, sell your possessions and give to the poor, and you will have treasure in heaven* (Matt 19:21). Here Jesus is addressing a sincerely religious young man who is desirous to have eternal life, to be in communion with God both in this life and the life to come. The young man claims to be perfect (= blameless) in terms of Jewish teaching and believes he has always kept the ten commandments and loved his neighbour as he loves himself. Yet he recognises that he still has not made it; there is something not quite right: he is lacking in some particular. So Jesus tells him what is missing. He must sell all he has, distribute the proceeds to the poor, and then follow Jesus. In other words he must give up all for the kingdom of God.

But what does *perfect* mean? It is spiritual and moral maturity – total commitment, entire consecration and wholehearted dedication to the kingdom of God and the Messiah, Jesus.

The young man, who was rich, could not bear the thought of losing his riches and, with sad face, went away. Later, Jesus explained why he had put this apparently impossible goal before the young man. 'With man this is impossible, but with God all things are possible' (v. 26). In other words, there is no limit to the help, mercy and grace which the eternal God can and will give to those who ask and are open to receive. The young man could be perfect – by grace.

b. *Be perfect as your heavenly Father is perfect* (Matt 5:48). This is from the Sermon on the Mount and occurs in a paragraph in which God's example is being presented. God makes his sun to shine on the evil and the good: and he sends the rain to fall upon the righteous and the unrighteous. His love and mercy, his compassion and kindness, extend to all, whatever be their moral state. Thus God's attitude and action are to be imitated by those who are his children. 'Love your enemies and pray for those who persecute you, that you may be sons of your Father in heaven' (5:44). The perfection here is the perfection of loving as God loves. She/he who exercises such perfect love (cf 1 John 4:18) will be a person (in terms of the beatitudes, Matt 5:1–11) who is poor in spirit, meek, merciful and pure in heart.

If the Gospel of Matthew contains the Sermon on the Mount, the Gospel of Luke contains the Sermon on the Plain (Luke 6:20–49). Here in verse 36 we read: 'Be merciful, just as your Father is merciful.' Again this occurs in a paragraph in which the kindness of God towards the ungrateful and wicked is emphasised; and, further, disciples have been urged to 'love your enemies, do good to them, and lend to them without expecting to get anything back' (v. 35). To be perfect is, at least, to be merciful.

We need to ponder this call to perfection carefully because the words of Jesus, 'Be perfect . . .', have been so influential in the Church over the centuries and in all geographical areas.

(i) First, let us take a look back into the Old Testament. Here we find that there are many calls to Israel to imitate God's character. They are particularly clear in the Book of Deuteronomy. Here is one which occurs in the context of a general call to obey God's commands, to love and to serve him:

And now, O Israel, what does the Lord your God ask of you but to fear the Lord your God, to walk in all his ways, to love him, to serve the Lord your God with all your heart and with all your soul and to observe the Lord's commands and decrees . . . For the Lord your God is God of gods and Lord of lords, the great God, mighty and awesome, who shows no partiality and accepts no bribes. He defends the cause of the fatherless and the widow, and loves the alien, giving him food and clothing. And you are to love those who are aliens, for you yourselves were aliens in Egypt . . . (10:12ff)

Here perfection includes both the imitation of God's mercy towards the fatherless, widow and alien (i.e. those with particular needs) and a life of fear (reverence), walking in God's way, loving and serving God, and obeying all his commandments.

(ii) In the second place, let us consider what following Jesus and walking in his way requires. To follow Jesus was not to be a student in a school run by a rabbi, where study of the ancient writings and attendance at lectures was the norm. To follow Jesus was practical in the sense that Jesus, like a master-craftsman, called men to be with him in order to follow and imitate. Discipleship was not matriculation in a College of Rabbis but apprenticeship in the kingdom of heaven. Bearing this in mind, we can note the following about walking in the way or following in the way of Jesus into perfection.

This way is one of *renunciation*. 'If anyone would come after me, he must deny himself and take up his cross and follow me' (Mark 8:34).

And, 'Any of you who does not give up everything he has cannot be my disciple' (Luke 14:33). Perfection here is via self-giving and suffering, and requires total surrender to Jesus as the King of the kingdom.

This way is one of *obedience*. 'Whoever does God's will is my brother and sister and mother' (Mark 3:35). And, 'Why do you call me "Lord, Lord," and do not do what I say?' Perfection is via the way of complete obedience to the will of God as revealed by Jesus.

This way is one of *humility*. 'If anyone wants to be first, he must be the very last, and the servant of all' (Mark 9:35). 'Whoever wants to become great among you must be your servant, and whoever wants to be first must be slave of all. For even the Son of Man did not come to be served, but to serve, and to give his life as a ransom for many' (Mark 10:43–44). Here we encounter perfection as the imitation of Jesus as the truly humble one – the one who says, 'I am among you as one who serves' (Luke 22:27), and 'Take my yoke upon you and learn from me, for I am gentle and humble in heart, and you will find rest for your souls' (Matt 11:29).

(iii) In the third place let us call to mind what we may call a spiritual law which operates in pure Science, the Arts, Music and Literature. Nothing truly enduring or really valuable is created and brought forth except by those whose aim is illimitable and whose standard is perfection. The true artist is such because he attempts more than he can ever achieve. The genuine poet is such because she attempts to say more than she can say. And the musician who is a composer is such because he attempts more than he can express. The moment the artist, poet and composer believe that their art is final in its accomplishment and the scientist holds that truth is perfect in his grasp, in that moment they cease to be what they claim to be.

So, also, in Christianity, the ultimate aim of the disciple of Jesus must be in its very nature illimitable. The perfection of God is eternal and infinite holy love and the disciple is called to imitate such a God. Thus the disciple will always be aiming for the highest and in so doing will (by the grace of God) achieve what is pleasing to his heavenly Father, day by day.

A man's reach should exceed his grasp
Or what's a heaven for . . . ? (Robert Browning)

(iv) Finally, we can now appreciate one reason why Jesus was so opposed to the religion of the Pharisees and Scribes. He had some very strong criticism to make of their interpretation and practice of Judaism (see, for example, his seven woes in Matthew 23). Not only was it legalistic and lacking compassion, it was also spiritually complacent. They were satisfied with their moral and spiritual achievements and did not feel the inner urge to press on to a deeper, closer and richer union with God. Absent from their spirituality was the longing for the courts of the Lord, the hungering and thirsting after righteousness and the desire to see the face of God.

And spiritual complacency is a sin that is never far away from any of us.

To summarise: Jesus set before his diciples the goal of perfection and offered the boundless grace of God as the source and strength of that perfection.

PAUL'S TEACHING ON PERFECTION AND MATURITY

In the King James Version we find that the word 'perfect' occurs more often in the Letters of Paul than it does in modern translations. They use other words instead – mature, complete and whole. This helps to make clear that Paul saw perfection in two different but complementary ways.

First of all, there is a perfection of human beings which is final and absolute, but it belongs only to the future kingdom of God in heaven. Putting this in terms of his personal pilgrimage, Paul wrote: 'But one thing I do: Forgetting what is behind and straining towards what is ahead, I press on towards the goal to win the prize for which God has called me heavenwards in Christ Jesus' (Phil 3:13–14). The picture in Paul's mind is that of the runner who knows how distracting a backward glance can be and who exerts every effort to press forward with the race. He seeks to run without swerving for he hastens to the goal, to Jesus Christ himself who is seated at the right hand of the Father in heaven: he seeks to attain to the resurrection of the dead, to fulness of life in an immortal body with a renewed heart, mind and will (v. 11).

Paul also spoke of this future perfection in his great hymn of love (1 Cor 13). 'When perfection comes, the imperfect disappears' he wrote. And continued: 'Now we see but a poor reflection: then we shall see [God-in-Christ] face to face. Now I know in part: then I shall know fully, even as I am fully known [by God].' To see God will be to experience everlastingly the love of God (13:13).

In the second place, there is a perfection which is relative when compared with the perfection which shall be in the age to come. This relative perfection can be called a maturity.

There is no doubt that Paul saw his work as an apostle not only to make converts for Jesus Christ but to lead the converts on (both as individuals and as societies of believers) to maturity of faith, hope and love. Not a maturity which has a final form but a maturity which always has a potential for growth toward God as long as the believer is alive.

Apparently, Paul thought of the growth within the Christian life in terms of human growth from infancy through childhood to adulthood. True adulthood is (relative) perfection. This is clear from his use of the word *teleios* in 1 Corinthians. First of all in 2:6 he claims that the apostles 'speak a message of wisdom among the mature' but the members of the church in Corinth were not yet ready for that wisdom. They were not spiritual and mature but worldly (3:1ff). Then in 14:20 he urges them in this manner: 'Brothers, stop thinking like children. In regard to evil be infants but in your thinking be adults.' They were to be mature and adult in their thinking. It is one thing to be childlike and another to be childish. The Corinthians were not employing their minds in the worship and service of Christ as they ought.

If we turn to the Letter to Colossae we meet this relative perfection in several contexts. Paul claimed that 'we proclaim Christ, admonishing everyone with all wisdom, so that we may present everyone perfect in Christ. To this end I labour, struggling with all his energy, which so powerfully works in me' (1:28–29). Here we can take *teleios* (perfect) to refer to the ultimate perfection, but in the context it is better translated/understood in terms of true maturity. Paul exerted all his energy and looked to God for help in order to present his converts to Christ as mature believers (in contrast to immature children).

The next example from Colossians is very much a corporate perfection/maturity. 'Therefore, as God's chosen people, holy and dearly loved, clothe yourselves with compassion, kindness, humility, gentleness and patience . . . And over all these virtues put on love, which binds them all together in perfect unity' (3:12–14). Here the word is *teleiotes* (perfect harmony). The maturity of a Christian community is seen when its members live together harmoniously by exercising the virtues, of which the most important is love.

The final example occurs in Paul's description of the prayers of Epaphras (see 1:7). 'Epaphras, who is one of you and a servant of Christ Jesus, sends greetings. He is always wrestling in prayer for you, that you may stand firm in all the will of God, mature and fully assured' (4:12). Here *teleios* (mature) means obeying God's will in practical living day by day so that they can stand firm against heresy and persecution and temptation. His prayer that they will be 'fully assured' may mean 'have clear convictions as to the essence of the gospel' or 'filled with a profound sense of God's grace and will'.

If we were to turn to the Letters to the Thessalonians we would meet much the same view of relative perfection/maturity. For example his prayer: 'May the Lord make your love increase and overflow for each other and for everyone else, just as ours does for you. May he strengthen you so that you will be blameless and holy in the presence of our God and Father when our Lord Jesus Christ comes with all his holy ones' (1, 3:12–13; see also 2, 4:6–8).

The perfection which was the goal of his ministry was one that admitted of continual growth: however, it was possible for him to say that some churches and some individual converts had actually reached a stage which could be called 'maturity' as compared with others who were as yet children in their Christian faith and duties. Yet that maturity which by the grace of God some had reached was not the top of the mountain but a staging post on the way up.

There is no spiritual complacency in Paul's doctrine of maturity. His own testimony is that of always needing to run the race, to fight the good fight, to press on towards the mark, to set his mind on things above, to reach out towards Christ in glory and to win Christ's commendation. Whatever depths of love he has experienced there is more to be experienced: and whatever heights of union with God he has reached there are yet greater heights to climb towards.

Yet Paul is clear that the first steps into maturity are reached by walking in the way of Christ, regenerated, guided, filled and inspired by the Holy Spirit, whom he calls the Spirit of Christ (Gal 5:16–18; Rom 8:9ff). In fact the task of the Holy Spirit, who comes in the name of Christ to continue and complete his work, is to form Christ in human hearts and to recreate souls in the perfect image of God (which Christ himself is – Col 1:15; 3:10; cf 2 Cor 4:4). Thus the goal of (relative) perfection or maturity (as also the goal of perfection in the gospels) may be expressed in terms of imitating Jesus.

Being indwelt by the Spirit, the believer is inspired to think, feel, desire, determine, speak and act like Jesus, perfect Man.

The imitation of Christ occurs both explicitly and implicitly as a theme in Paul's Letters. Here are some explicit examples:

> We who are strong ought to bear with the failings of the weak and not to please ourselves. Each of us should please his neighbour for his good, to build him up. For even Christ did not please himself . . . (Rom 15:1–4)

> Your attitude should be the same as that of Christ Jesus . . . (Phil 2:5)

> Be imitators of God, therefore, as dearly loved children and live a life of love, just as Christ loved us and gave himself up for us as a fragrant offering and sacrifice to God. (Eph 5:1–2)

We may reflect upon the fact that to imitate God/Jesus is to reach both for relative perfection (a maturity which becomes more mature) and final perfection (which itself admits of a growth from glory unto glory).

Spirituality, we may conclude, is all about moving from a condition of immaturity to maturity and imperfection to perfection in the imitation of Jesus. The Greek word *teleios* derives from *telos*, meaning goal or end: there should be no standing still.

7

Be Holy

The call to be holy is consistently heard throughout the whole Bible. So also is the call to be sanctified. And the reason for this pervasive and persistent call is that the Lord God, Father, Son and Holy Spirit, is 'the Holy One'. The heavenly choir forever sing: 'Holy, holy, holy is the Lord God Almighty, who was, and is, and is to come' (Rev 4:8, echoing Isa 6:3).

One of the most important statements both in the Old and New Testaments is this: 'Be holy, because I am holy' (1 Pet 1:16, citing Lev 19:2). The holiness of God is his singular and radiant majesty, his absolute purity and perfect righteousness. And, since we are made in the image and likeness of God, we are to imitate his holiness, to be holy as is truly appropriate for a child of God to be. In other words, to be holy, even as Jesus was/is holy.

To put some content in this divine command to imitate the holiness of God we need to examine briefly the concept of holiness in the Old Testament, before turning to the New. However, before doing this, it is perhaps necessary to recall that though we are dealing with two groups of words – holy/holiness and sanctify/sanctification – there is both in the Old and New Testaments only one basic group (having one stem). In the New this is *hagi* (so *hagios* = holy; *hagiazō* = I sanctify) and in the Old this is *qds* (so *qados* = holy; *qadas* = to hallow). We get the word holy/holiness from Old English and sanctify/sanctification from the Latin.

THE OLD TESTAMENT

Here the idea of sanctification (being holy or made holy) has particular reference to the coming before God in worship at the sanctuary or holy place. Those who are to meet God are to cleanse themselves by washing body and garments. This is well illustrated in Exodus 19. The tribes of Israel are camped before Mount Sinai where God is to reveal his will for Israel to Moses. Sanctification includes washing of garments, abstaining from sexual relations, not touching the mountain where God reveals his glory, and maintaining a state of watchfulness. Though the emphasis is apparently on external purity underlying it is an internal preparation to receive the content of God's covenant.

Together with the idea of cleansing, holiness means being dedicated or consecrated to God and his service. Thus the special places and implements used in divine worship are holy – holy temple, holy altar, holy (sabbath) day, holy sacrifices/offerings and holy furnishings (see the book of Leviticus). Further, the priesthood, being set apart for God's service in the sanctuary, is also holy (Lev 21:7).

However, as we have indicated, holiness and sanctification do not consist only in external purity and dedication. In the laws found in Leviticus the command to be externally cleansed is found alongside the command to obey God's moral laws (see, for example, the so-called Holiness Code in Lev 19ff). And purity of heart is much emphasised in the psalms:

Create in me a pure heart, O God,
   and renew a steadfast spirit within me. (51:10)

and:

Who may ascend the hill of the Lord?
   Who may stand in his holy place?
He who has clean hands and a pure heart,
   who does not lift up his soul to an idol
   or swear by what is false. (24:3–4)

It is also a constant theme in the message of the prophets:

'Even now', declares the Lord, 'return to me with all your
heart, with fasting and weeping and mourning.' Rend your
heart and not your garments. Return to the Lord your God
for he is gracious and compassionate, slow to anger and
abounding in love . . . Blow the trumpet in Zion, declare a
holy fast, call a sacred assembly. (Joel 2:12–16)

Here the holy is presented both as embracing the external and
the internal – purity of heart and dedication to the service and
worship of the Lord.

We also find in the Old Testament an insistence that all true
holiness and sanctification is inspired by and brought into being
by the holy Lord himself. He is the One who sets Israel apart
by his election and choice of them (Ex 31:13; Lev 21:23; 22:9,
16). So though Israelites are to sanctify themselves through
self-dedication and service, that dedication and service is only
possible through the guidance and strength of the holy Lord.

THE NEW TESTAMENT

Here we find that though there are a few echoes of the cultic
meaning of sanctification (e.g. Matt 23:19) and of the idea of
consecration to God (1 Cor 7:14; 1 Tim 4:5), the prominent
and decisive meaning is moral. 'Without holiness no-one will
see the Lord' (Heb 12:14) complements, 'Blessed are the pure
in heart for they shall see God' (Matt 5:5).

In fact, holiness is defined with reference to Jesus Christ and
to the Holy Spirit, who is the Spirit of Christ. Jesus is the 'holy
One' not only because he was wholly consecrated to God's
service as the Messiah but also (and more importantly) because
he was filled and constantly re-filled with the Holy Spirit. The
Holy Spirit was the source in him not only of ministerial gifts
but also of meekness and lowliness of heart/mind.

The Holy Spirit continues to fill his human nature as he lives
in heaven. Raised from the dead by the Spirit of holiness (Rom
1:4) and exalted into heaven in his glorified human
body/nature, Jesus is still filled (and as Man is continually being
filled) with the Holy Spirit. Thus he remains the One – the

Holy One – from and through whom the Holy Spirit goes forth to act in and upon those who believe the good news of salvation. God the Father sends the Holy Spirit via the Lord Jesus to the world: so the Spirit descends and works among human beings as the Spirit of Christ, bearing his name and distributing his power, virtues and characteristics. All this was explained by Jesus in his long talk to the disciples on the eve of his crucifixion (John 14–16).

We may say that Christ the Lord acts through the Spirit and in the world in two complementary ways. First of all, he bestows spiritual gifts upon the Church – apostles, prophets, evangelists, pastors and teachers, along with speaking in tongues, interpretation of tongues, prophecy, words of wisdom and knowledge, power to perform miracles and power to believe against all the odds (see 1 Cor 12 and Eph 4:1–16). These very special – in some cases supernatural – gifts are given not for personal benefit but for spiritual growth in holiness, for ministry, and for edification of all the believing fellowship.

In the second place (and this is our particular concern) Christ the Lord acts through the Holy Spirit to bring sinners to repentance and faith and then, following spiritual birth/conversion, into a life of consecration to God's service and purity of mind, heart and will. The special work of the Spirit in leading sinners to faith in Jesus is described in John 16:7–11. He will convict the world of guilt in regard to sin, righteousness and judgement.

At regeneration (birth from/by the Spirit) God begins the work of recreating the soul in the image of God, according to the model which is Christ. As the Holy Spirit lives in heart and mind he leads believers not only to rejoice in God and his salvation, but also to mortify sinful desires, resist temptation and consecrate the whole self to the Lord Jesus. And, as the Holy Spirit does his work of purification and renewal, he also brings spiritual gifts from the exalted Lord Jesus.

In fact we learn from the New Testament that the past, present and future tenses of the verb *hagiazō* (to sanctify/make holy) apply to the people of God who trust in Christ. In union with the Lord Jesus by faith through the Holy Spirit, believers are declared to be both righteous (justified) and holy (sanctified). God the Father, seeing them not in their moral uncleanness but in the purity of Christ, reckons them to be holy. 'Christ Jesus . . . is our righteousness, holiness and redemption' (1 Cor 1:30); 'You were washed, you were sanctified, you were justified in the name of the Lord Jesus Christ and by the Spirit of our God' (1 Cor 6:11). The knowledge of this union and of how God the Father estimates it ought to be the basis of a complete consecration to God's will day by day. What God judges we are in Christ we are by the Spirit to become.

Thus, for the present time believers are called to be holy. The position is explained by Paul in the opening of several of his Letters. For example: 'To the church of God in Corinth, to those sanctified in Christ Jesus, and called to be holy . . .' (1 Cor 1:2). In the first of his Letters he wrote: 'It is God's will that you should be holy' (1 Thess 4:3–4) and went on to explain how this means practical, moral purity. And near the end of that Letter he offered this prayer for present and future: 'May God himself, the God of peace, sanctify you through and through. May your whole spirit, soul and body be kept blameless at the coming of the Lord Jesus Christ. The one who calls you is faithful and he will do it' (1 Thess 5:23–24). In a later Letter, after describing the great promises of grace, he wrote: 'Since we have these promises, dear friends, let us purify ourselves from everything that contaminates body and spirit, perfecting holiness out of reverence for God' (2 Cor 7:1).

Finally, holiness is the goal to which the whole Church of God moves. 'Praise be to God the Father of our Lord Jesus Christ, who has blessed us in the heavenly realms with every spiritual blessing in Christ. For he chose us in him before the creation of the world to be holy and blameless in his sight . . .' (Eph 1:3–4). Thus 'Christ loved the church and gave himself up for her, to make her holy, cleansing her by the washing of water through the word, and to present her to himself as a radiant church, without stain or wrinkle or any other blemish, but holy and blameless' (Eph 5:25–27). In fact the hope within the gospel is that you will be presented holy and blameless and free from all accusation in and by Christ to the Father (Col 1:22–23). There is no possibility whatsoever that the wicked will enter the kingdom of God in the age to come (1 Cor 6:9–11), for without holiness no one will see the Lord.

Holiness as a goal of the Christian life is that moral and spiritual quality we see in the Lord Jesus Christ. And this begins when the Holy Spirit comes to dwell in the soul and sanctify the whole personality. But this beginning is but a seed and this seed has to grow so that the soul is re-created, renewed and refashioned as the old ego is gradually eliminated. Only with resurrection of the body will the individual soul reach that final goal of holiness and be able to see the glory of God in the face of Jesus Christ in the perfection of heaven.

8

Be Righteous

One of the fundamental characteristics of authentic Protestantism – be it Presbyterian, Lutheran, Anglican, Baptist or Methodist – is the insistence that 'we are justified by faith'. This is shorthand for 'we are declared and accounted righteous in God's heavenly court through the reckoning to us of the righteousness of the Lord Jesus Christ, in whom we believe and trust'. And it is based upon the clear teaching of St Paul particularly in his letter to Rome. There we read that 'Jesus our Lord was delivered over to death for our sins and was raised to life for our justification' (4:25) and 'we are justified freely by his grace through the redemption that came by Christ Jesus' (3:24) and 'we maintain that a man is justified by faith apart from observing the law' (3:28).

THE OLD TESTAMENT

Paul's teaching is developed from the Old Testament by the guidance of the Holy Spirit as he reflected upon the saving work of the Lord Jesus. There we find that to call God righteous is not, in the first place, to speak of his essence or being as God: it is rather to speak of his attitude to and relationship with Israel, his covenant people. He always acts rightly towards them sending them blessing or judgement, according to the terms of his gracious covenant. 'You are always righteous, O Lord' confessed Jeremiah (12:1). However, because by nature God is full of mercy and grace, his righteousness will include, Isaiah prophesied, sending his great salvation to his people, even though they break his covenant and do not deserve any mercy. In fact salvation becomes a synonym for righteousness: 'I am bringing my righteousness near; it is not far away; and my salvation will not be delayed. I will grant salvation to Zion, my splendour to Israel' (46:13). Paul developed the theme of God's righteousness becoming his provision of salvation.

With regard to the Israelites, righteousness refers to being in and maintaining a right relationship with the Lord their God, with his Law, and with fellow human beings. When viewed in the strictest terms and by the highest standards, the truth of the matter is that Israel was not righteous: 'All have turned aside, they have become corrupt; there is no-one who does good, not even one' (Ps 14:3; 53:3; cited by Paul in Rom 3:10–12). However, individual Israelites did seek to fulfil their covenant obligations to God and fellow Israelites and they are called 'righteous' (e.g. Ps 33:1; 119:121; 146:8). We have to describe this as a relative righteousness for when the full extent of the heart, mind and will are open before God the real truth is 'no-one living is righteous before you' (Ps 143:2).

Not only did the prophets look forward to the display of God's righteousness as salvation for Israel, they also spoke of a future anointed servant of the Lord (Messiah) of the lineage of king David, who would lead his people, Israel, into God's salvation. In describing the future Messiah, the word 'righteous' is often used or implied. For example, in Isaiah 11 the future descendant of David is described as being the one upon whom the Spirit of the Lord will rest and:

> He will not judge by what he sees with his eyes,
>   or decide by what he hears with his ears;
> but with righteousness he will judge the needy,
>   with justice he will give decisions for the poor of the
>   earth.
> He will strike the earth with the rod of his mouth;
>   with the breath of his lips he will slay the wicked.
> Righteousness will be his belt and faithfulness the sash
>   around his waist. (vv 3–5)

Again Paul developed this theme of the Messiah as the embodiment and the bringer to mankind of God's saving righteousness.

PAUL'S TEACHING

Jesus is this Messiah. As our Substitute and Representative Jesus not only perfectly obeyed the covenant/law of God on our behalf but he also bore the penalty due to us for having broken God's law – as Isaiah had prophesied (52:13 – 52:12) concerning the suffering of God's righteous servant. Therefore there is a gospel to proclaim: there is forgiveness and acceptance with God: there is justification – being declared and accounted righteous for Christ's sake – in God's presence. The power and thrill of this message throbs through the early chapters of the Letter to Rome.

However, the fact that Paul taught that God's righteousness as salvation in and through Jesus, the Messiah, is received in faith and trust is not to be understood as suggesting that to be righteous/just in daily living is of no consequence. He vehemently rejected the very suggestion that since God's grace is so rich and freely available we could sin the more to receive the more grace. 'Shall we go on sinning, so that grace may increase? By no means! We died to sin (with and in Christ in his death); how can we live in it any longer?' (6:1–2). And he proceeded:

> Count yourselves dead to sin but alive to God in Christ Jesus. Therefore do not let sin reign in your mortal body so that you obey its evil desires. Do not offer the parts of your body to sin, as instruments of wickedness, but rather offer yourselves to God, as those who have been brought from death to life; and offer the parts of your body to him as instruments of righteousness. For sin shall not be your master, because you are not under law but under grace. (6:11–14)

In other words justified sinners have a new Master who is the embodiment and personification of all that is right and they are to serve him wholeheartedly and without any hesitation or reserve. Paul had no doubts for he repeated himself to say: 'You have been set free from sin and have become slaves to righteousness' (6:18).

But how are sinners who are accounted righteous to offer their whole selves as instruments of righteousness and be actual slaves of righteousness? The answer is provided by Paul in chapter eight. Not only has God the Father sent his Son to fulfil for us 'the righteous requirements of the law' (8:4) but he has poured out his Spirit upon us for the sake of his Son. In the strength and by the guidance of the Spirit we are to live righteously – in a right relationship of loving communion with our God and in right relationships with God's creation. The latter means imitating the Lord Jesus in his attitude to fellow human beings. Our aim each day is to die to sin and to live righteously, aiming for the highest understanding and expression of God's righteousness in our lives. It is a struggle at times but Christ is on our side (Rom 8:10)!

We aim to be righteous now because we are slaves of Jesus, the Righteous One, and because we shall be truly righteous in mind, heart, will and body in the life of the age to come. 'Through the obedience of the one man (Jesus) the many will be made righteous' (5:19). God has not only accounted those in union with his Son to be righteous, he intends that we aim now to be righteous and certainly after the Second Coming of Jesus to earth we will finally be made righteous. Paul took up this theme in the Letter to Philippi:

> I consider everything a loss compared to the surpassing greatness of knowing Christ Jesus my Lord, for whose sake I have lost all things. I consider them rubbish, that I may gain Christ and be found in him, not having a righteousness of my own that comes from the law, but that which is through faith in Christ – the righteousness that comes from God and is by faith. I want to know Christ and the power of his resurrection and the fellowship of sharing in his sufferings, becoming like him in death, and so, somehow, to attain to the resurrection of the dead. (3:8–11)

Justification by faith is a glorious truth: but it is the beginning of a fervent desire and wholehearted commitment to be made righteous in mind and body. To be justified (Old English = rightwised) is to become just (righteous) and to aim to be like

Jesus, the Just/Righteous One. 'Be righteous because Christ is your righteousness.'

IN THE GOSPELS

The gracious justification of sinners by God is taught in the Gospels, particularly in the parable told by Jesus of the tax-collector and Pharisee who went up to the Temple to pray (Luke 19:9–14). The penitent tax-collector who prayed, 'God be merciful' went home 'justified'.

And the call to be just/righteous is a constant theme in the Gospels, especially that of Matthew. Jesus is portrayed as often rejecting the apparent righteousness of the Jewish religious leaders for it is incomplete, even hypocritical. Further, it is only external, having to do with outward performance of duties and not involving the custody of the heart and mind. In solemn words Jesus spoke to them saying: 'Woe to you, teachers of the law and Pharisees, you hypocrites! You are like white-washed tombs, which look beautiful on the outside but on the inside are full of dead men's bones and everything unclean. In the same way, on the outside you appear to people as righteous but on the inside you are full of hypocrisy and wickedness' (Matt 23:27–28). Though they seemed to be in a right relationship with the law of God they were in fact breaking it in their hearts.

Jesus expected his disciples to aim high. 'Seek first the kingdom of God and his righteousness' (Matt 6:33); 'Blessed are those who hunger and thirst after righteousness' (Matt 5:6), and 'Unless your righteousness surpasses that of the Pharisees and the teachers of the law, you certainly will not enter the kingdom of heaven' (Matt 5:20). In fact the Sermon on the Mount in Matthew and the Sermon on the Plain in Luke provide a full account of what it is to be righteous, to do righteousness/justice and thereby to walk humbly with God. And the portrayal of final judgement by Christ at the end of the age in the vision of the Son of Man separating the sheep and goats (Matt 25:31–46) clearly teaches that the righteousness of those who inherit the kingdom of God will be one that is found in attitude and action. 'Whatever you did for the least of these brothers of mine, you did for me' Jesus will say to those who have freely loved the needy in righteous behaviour.

Following the judgement by the Son of Man, God will establish righteousness as the characteristic of the new age. 'Then the righteous will shine like the sun in the kingdom of their Father' (Matt 13:43). Those who are declared righteous are to live righteously, longing for the perfect righteousness of the kindom of heaven.

REFLECTIONS

Protestants have usually spoken of the Christian life in terms of having been justified by faith and being sanctified by the Holy Spirit (see further my book, *Justification and Sanctification*, 1983) This is, of course, correct as far as it goes. However, as we have seen, the verb *hagiazō* (to make holy, to sanctify) and the verb *dikaioō* (to justify, to rightwise) are used in the past, present and future tenses.

1. In Christ we have been, therefore in God's sight we are, both sanctified and justified.
2. In Christ we are being made holy/saintly and righteous/just through the influence of the indwelling Holy Spirit.
3. Through, in and with Christ we shall be made fully holy and righteous, true saints and really just, at the resurrection of the body for life in the age to come.

Thus the call to be holy and the call to be righteous are different but complementary emphases within one general aim and direction. If holiness and sanctity are all about being pure in heart and wholly consecrated to God, then righteousness and justice are all about being in right relationships and doing what is right for Christ's sake.

9

Be Godly

To be described as godly, pious, devout and religious is not necessarily welcomed by the modern Christian. These terms seem to have an old-fashioned ring about them: they bring to mind 'strict Puritanism', 'Victorian values', 'tough personal discipline', 'lack of freedom', 'Sabbatarianism', 'solid reliability', and 'self-reliance'. Joy seems to be absent from them!

Our investigation would, however, be incomplete if we did not recognise (1) their important place in the vocabulary of the Church over the centuries, and (2) their roots in the Bible. Let us begin with the latter.

IN SCRIPTURE

The Greek word which translators render as godliness, piety, devotion and religion is *eusebeia*. The basic meaning of this word relates to the reverence or fear of God – having a right attitude towards one's holy, Creator, Judge and Redeemer. We recall that the 'fear of the Lord' is a very important aspect of a right relationship to God within the Old Testament – see e.g. Ps 2:11; 19:9; 22:23. The word *eusebeia* is used quite often in 1 and 2 Timothy and 2 Peter and so we shall take our examples from these Letters. Here are five:

(i) Giving instructions to his younger brother in Christ, Paul said to Timothy:

Have nothing to do with godless myths and old wives' tales;

rather, train yourself *to be godly*. For physical training is of some value, but *godliness* has value for all things, holding promise for both the present life and the life to come. (1 Tim 4:7–8)

The modern American Roman Catholic translation, the NAB, renders the first as *life of piety* and the second as *discipline of religion*.

The meaning of *eusebeia* is reasonably clear, however we translate it. It is that which is gained (with God's help) through spiritual (in contrast to physical) training. It is being blameless in attitude and conduct towards God our Father. And as the TEV renders, *eusebeia* 'is valuable in every way because it promises life both for the present and for the future'.

(ii) As a general principle Paul laid down that:

Godliness with contentment is great gain. (1 Tim 6:6)

The NAB offers *religion* (and so do the NEB and JB).

The person with the inner resources of faith, hope and love has soul-sufficiency: she/he is not desirous of external possessions recognising (as 6:7 states) that 'we brought nothing into the world and we can take nothing out of it'. Godliness here is living by faith, trusting God, hoping for the fulfilment of his promises and loving him and his creation.

(iii) Speaking of the days immediately before the Second Coming of Jesus Christ to earth, to judge the world, Paul said the following:

There will be terrible times in the last days. People will be lovers of themselves . . . treacherous, rash, conceited, lovers of pleasure rather than lovers of God – having the form of *godliness* but denying its power. (2 Tim 3:1–5)

The NAB renders 'as they make a pretense of *religion* but negate its power'. People will have all the outward trappings of religious practice – say their prayers, read their Bibles, use the language of Sion, and so on – but the inward reality of souls impelled by faith, hope and love will be missing.

(iv) Writing of that which the Lord Jesus Christ provides for the inner life of his disciples, Peter explained:

> His divine power has given us everything we need for life and *godliness* through our knowledge of him who called us by his own glory and goodness. (2 Pet 1:3)

The NAB renders as 'everything necessary for a life of genuine *piety*'.

In union with (i.e. true knowledge of) Jesus Christ the believer has everything she/he needs (not would like) for everlasting life and for true, inward faith, hope and love. This need is well supplied by Jesus through the Holy Spirit.

(v) Speaking of the judgement of God upon the present physical universe, Peter drew this conclusion from the divine intervention through the Second Coming of Jesus:

> Since everything will be destroyed in this way, what kind of people ought we to be? You ought to live holy and *godly lives*, as you look forward to the day of God and speed its coming. (2 Pet 3:11)

The NAB renders 'holy in your conduct and *devotion*'. Perhaps Peter is seeking to cover both the 'inner' and 'outer' lives, using holiness for purity in word and action and godliness/devotion for inner purity of thought, desire and intention.

So we see that *eusebeia* describes the inner life of the soul – mind, heart and will – directed (in the power of the Holy Spirit) towards the Lord Jesus in faith, hope and love (see Tit 2:12).

IN THE CHURCH

We must now turn to the use of the words godliness, piety, devotion and religion in the Church. We shall discover that they are all used with reference to spirituality: specifically to that to which spirituality is aimed. Let us begin with 'religion'.

1. *Religion*. In the Roman Catholic Church there is a long tradition of calling those who enter a monastery or convent by the noun 'religious'. It is said that they have entered into religion, meaning they are seeking *eusebeia* – to be truly and inwardly godly, devout and pious.

The word has also been used by Protestants as the equivalent of godliness and holiness. An important example is the title of the book by Philip Doddridge to which we have already made reference – *The Rise and Progress of Religion in the Soul*. It covers such topics as genuine conversion to God; repentance, faith, hope and love; testing, temptation and suffering; meditation and prayer and receiving the sacraments; and the right approach to death and true usefulness while on earth.

In the much loved and widely used *Book of Common Prayer* (1662) 'religion' is used in prayers; 'O Lord, we beseech thee to keep thy Church and household continually in thy true religion . . .' (Epiphany 5) and 'Grant unto all them that are admitted into the fellowship of Christ's religion, that they may eschew those things that are contrary to their profession, and follow all such things as are agreeable to the same . . .' (Easter 3) and 'Graft into our hearts the love of thy name, increase in us true religion, nourish us with all goodness . . .' (Trinity 7).

2. *Devotion*. When used by modern Christians this noun is often used in the plural, *devotions*, and refers to an act of worship which will include hymns, Bible reading, prayers and an address. In this sense devotions are an expression of devotion.

In both Roman Catholic and Protestant teaching on the spiritual life, devotion has to do with an entire consecration of oneself to God (literally, making a vow of one's whole self to

God). Here is an explanation of devotion by John Nicholas Grou (1713–1803):

> True and solid devotion is that disposition of the heart by which we are ready to do and to suffer, without exception or reserve, everything which comes from God's good pleasure, everything which is the will of God. And this disposition is the most excellent of all the gifts of the Holy Spirit . . .
>
> Devotion is something most interior and which has to do with the inmost life of the soul, for it affects that within us which is most spiritual: that is to say, our understanding and our will. Devotion consists, then, neither in reasoning, nor in imagination, nor in anything we can seize by our senses . . . The principle of devotion is, that God being the one source and the one author of holiness, the reasonable creature ought to depend upon him in everything, and be absolutely governed by the Spirit of God. We must be always attached to God in the depths of our souls, always attentive to his voice within us, always faithful to accomplish what he asks of us each moment. (*Manual for Interior Souls*, new ed. 1955, pp 1–2)

And of course, many books on spirituality have in their titles the word 'devout'. There is the famous English study by William Law, *A Serious Call to a Devout and Holy Life* (1728) and the even more widely read *Introduction to the Devout Life*, by Francis de Sales (which I have recently edited in a paperback edition for Protestants).

3. *Piety*. One of the influential books of the English Reformation was *The Practice of Piety* (1610) by Lewis Bayly, Bishop of Bangor. By 1735 it was in its fifty-ninth English edition. Piety was godliness: not formal Christianity, but religion with spiritual power and lively faith.

This positive meaning of piety was much used in Germany with reference to what has come to be called the Pietist Movement within the Lutheran Church. It was a revival of vital religion and joyful godliness in the context of the nominal and formal worship and practice of the State Church. One of the important books of the movement was entitled *Pia Desideria* (1675) meaning 'Pious Wishes' (for the renewal of the Church and inner renewal of Christians) and its author was Philip Jacob Spener.

The two Wesley brothers, John and Charles, were influenced by the Pietist Movement (through the Moravians) and they used piety in a positive way. In the preface to the first edition of *A Collection of Hymns for the use of the People called Methodists* (1780), there is a preface by John Wesley, and its last paragraph reads thus:

> That which is of infinitely more moment than the spirit of poetry is the spirit of piety. And I trust, all persons of real judgment will find this breathing through the whole Collection. It is in this view chiefly that I would recommend it to every truly pious reader, as a means of raising or quickening the spirit of devotion; of confirming his faith; of enlivening his hope; and of kindling and increasing his love to God and man. When Poetry thus keeps its place as the handmaid of Piety, it shall attain not a poor perishable wreath but a crown that fadeth not away.

It may be claimed on behalf of the successive Methodist Hymnbooks that they present the longing and aiming for perfection, piety and devotion in more compelling terms than any other hymn book.

4. *Godliness*. In the most important of all Anglican books of theology, *Of the Laws of Ecclesiastical Polity* (1597), Richard Hooker provided a comment on godliness which was shared by all Protestants and Roman Catholics of his time. He wrote: 'Godliness is the chiefest top and wellspring of all true virtues, even as God is of all good things' (Book V, chap.1, sec.2). His meaning is that God alone is the origin and source of all that is truly good: and godliness (= true religion) is the highest expression as well as the true source of all genuine virtues.

In the *Book of Common Prayer*, the prayer for Trinity 22 begins: 'Lord, we beseech thee to keep thy household, the Church, in continual godliness . . . devoutly given to serve thee in good works . . .' And the prayer for the following Sunday is: 'O God, our refuge, our strength, who art the author of all godliness . . .'

And in the preface to the 1876 edition of the *Methodist Hymnbook* we read these moving words:

> Well does it become all the lovers of Scriptural Christianity, but especially the Methodists, to be thankful to God, the Author of every good gift for the endowments and labours of Charles Wesley, which were so long and faithfully conse-crated to the promotion of vital and experimental religion, and by which the 'power of godliness' which it is the mission of Methodism to spread, has been alike exemplified and vindicated . . .

Here we encounter not only the evangelical use of 'godliness' as practical holiness and righteousness but also the specifically evangelical emphasis upon 'vital and experimental religion' – that is, religion that is truly experienced as the power and love of God in the heart.

So, in summary, we may say that spirituality is related to religion, devotion, piety and godliness as the road to London is related to London itself. Spirituality is all about travelling in vital religion, true devotion, lively piety and the power of godli-ness to God in and with and through Jesus Christ.

PART THREE

Fulfilling Every Duty

10

Open to God

It is one thing to be told, on the authority of Scripture: 'This is the Goal: here is what you should be like as a Christian.' But it is another to find the motivation to aim for the highest and to know how to proceed to the ideal of holiness.

In the last analysis, it may be asked: Is the whole matter reduced to grit, guts and determination, rigorous self-discipline and total dedication? Is it as if God places us at baptism/conversion on a road, shows us the way, and says, 'Be resolute. Go on the narrow way without turning left or right until you arrive at the gates of the heavenly kingdom. There you will find a royal welcome'.

Or, on the other hand, is the whole matter reduced to the sovereign grace of God and the mighty power of the Holy Spirit? Is it as if God places us at baptism/conversion in a boat, hoists the sails, and then sends the wind to blow us unfailingly in the right direction to arrive on the shores of the celestial city; and he says, 'Sit still, trust in me and you will arrive safely in the harbour of the heavenly kingdom'.

TWO ASPECTS

Within the New Testament there are statements of Jesus (and his apostles) which can be lifted out of their context, placed alongside each other, and used to support each of these opposing interpretations.

Take, first of all, the teaching that by valiant and dedicated effort and striving we can arrive at the Goal. Jesus said:

77

Make every effort to enter through the narrow door because many, I tell you, many will try to enter and will not be able to do. (Luke 13:24)

Anyone who does not carry his cross and follow me cannot be my disciple. (Luke 14:27)

Everyone who exalts himself will be humbled and he who humbles himself will be exalted. (Luke 18:14)

No-one who puts his hand to the plough and looks back is fit for service in the kingdom of God. (Luke 9:62)

And the apostle Paul urged the young man, Timothy, in these terms:

But you, man of God flee from all this (evil), and pursue righteousness, godliness, faith, love, endurance and gentleness. Fight the good fight of the faith. Take hold of the eternal life to which you were called when you made your good confession in the presence of many witnesses. (1 Tim 6:11–12)

Timothy is to 'flee', 'pursue', 'fight', and 'take hold'.

Take, in the second place, the teaching that we are wholly dependent upon the sovereign grace of God through Jesus and in the power of the Holy Spirit. Jesus said:

I praise you, Father, Lord of heaven and earth, because you have hidden these things from the wise and learned, and revealed them to little children. Yes, Father, for this was your good pleasure. (Luke 10:21)

Do not be afraid, little flock, for your Father has been pleased to give you the kingdom. (Luke 12:32)

Apart from me, you can do nothing. (John 15:5)

When the Spirit of Truth comes, he will guide you into all truth. He will not speak on his own, he will speak only what he hears, and he will tell you what is yet to come. (John 16:13)

And the apostle Paul told the church in Ephesus:

> It is by grace you have been saved, through faith – and this is not from yourselves, it is the gift of God – not by works, so that no-one can boast. For we are God's workmanship, created in Christ Jesus to do good works, which God prepared in advance for us to do. (Eph 2:8–10)

The 'saints in Ephesus' who are the 'faithful in Christ Jesus' (1.1) are to remember that salvation is by grace alone. Paul told the Philippians that God 'who began a good work in you will carry it on to completion until the day of Christ Jesus' (1:6).

THE PARADOX OF GRACE

Can we reconcile these two apparently opposing dimensions? The answer is 'yes' if we bear in mind that we are not dealing with two equal powers. Human beings at their noblest are never more than dependent creatures, to whom God gives life and being. Their best efforts will never come anywhere near the perfect actions of their eternal Creator, Sustainer and Father. In fact, as creatures and servants of God, we must say (after doing everything we were told to do): 'We are unworthy servants; we have only done our duty' (Luke 17:10).

In comparison with his fallible creatures, the Lord is perfect in nature and being, thought and word, will and action. And as Creator and Father he calls his creatures into communion with himself so that he is truly their God and they are really his people. He always – because of who he is, the Lord – must take the initiative and ultimately be in control. Yet, because he has made mankind in his own image, in his likeness, we are able to make a *genuine* response to his invitation and truly obey his word. Never forgetting that he is always Lord, we are called to give ourselves unreservedly, wholeheartedly, single mindedly and devotedly to him and his cause.

We see how God took the initiative and called for human response in the ministry of Jesus. First, God so loved the world that he gave his only-begotten Son. Then, as incarnate Son, Jesus proclaimed the arrival of the kingdom of God (the rule of God bringing salvation). It was like a great army at the city gates waiting to enter (Mk 1:15). Therefore, his hearers were to submit to God's rule and receive his salvation: they were to live as true disciples of the kingdom, looking forward to a glorious future, and not being put off by problems, testing, temptations and trials (see the Sermon on the Mount, Matt 5–7). So in the four Gospels we have two sides of the divine coin of grace: on the one is the emphasis on the free and sovereign grace of God in Jesus; and, on the other, is the call for nothing less than total submission and obedience to this Lord.

The teaching of Paul supports what we find in the Gospels, and it may be described as the paradox of grace. Here are some of his statements which contain both the emphasis on God's grace and upon human endeavour:

> If you live according to the sinful nature, you will die; but if by the Spirit you put to death the misdeeds of the body, you will live, because those who are led by the Spirit of God are sons of God. (Rom 8:13–14)

> But the Lord said to me, 'My grace is sufficient for you, for my power is made perfect by weakness'. Therefore I will boast all the more gladly about my weaknesses, so that Christ's power may rest on me . . . For when I am weak, then I am strong'. (2 Cor 12:9–10)

> Therefore, my dear friends, as you have always obeyed [me] – not only in my presence but now much more in my absence – continue to work out your salvation with fear and trembling, for it is God who works in you to will and to act according to his good purpose. (Phil 2:12–13)

> I know what it is to be in need, and I know what it is to have plenty. I have learned the secret of being content in any and every situation, whether well fed or hungry. I can do everything through the Lord who gives me strength. (Phil 4:12–13)

Paul's life as well as his teaching contains both emphases. He always feels entirely dependent upon the grace of our Lord Jesus Christ: and he always strives to give of his very best in serving the Lord Jesus Christ. It is certainly 'all of grace' but it is also a 'total dedication in mind, heart, will and body'. However, the latter is only possible because of the former.

FULFILLING THE AIM

Christian spirituality accepts not only that God has set before his people a goal [Part Two] at which to aim, but also that he has provided, provides and will provide for them all the help needed to fulfil this aim. However, spirituality leaves to theology the exposition of the nature and content of this divine help; it concentrates upon that side of the divine coin which consists of the duties of believers as they respond to God's grace. Such duties as submission, meditation, prayer, attending corporate worship and receiving Holy Communion are some of the areas which spirituality covers.

Further, a spiritual guide takes each of these duties and offers practical guidance as to means, methods and ways of fulfilling them. For example, suggestions as to how to meditate, forms of prayer, ways of cultivating the virtues and methods of self-examination have been, and still are, offered. And the guidance can be given in general terms or specifically, depending upon circumstances. And we must always bear in mind, and never forget, that all ways, means and methods are never to be ends in themselves but only routes towards the true end – fellowship and union with God. It is also worth adding that experiences gained in fulfilling duties are not to be ends in themselves but only indications of the greater experience which comes to those who, being pure of heart, see God in his glory.

In fact the variety of duties may be compared to the variety of tasks required in the proper cultivation and care of a garden. The gardener recognises that her garden is wholly dependent upon the sunshine, the rain and the multitude of chemical reactions which take place (the nitrogen cycle etc.). Yet she has to dig, to hoe, to weed, to plant, to transplant, to prune, to mow and to harvest. If she did not maintain constant vigilance and work, the garden would soon get out of shape and become a wilderness. In the cultivation of mind, heart and will we are totally dependent upon God's grace but yet we have to be as a good gardener of the soul, sowing and reaping, pruning and weeding, digging and transplanting. The aim is that the fruit of the Spirit will grow and be seen and tasted.

In the next three chapters we shall explore the basic duties of spirituality in general terms. The structure in which we shall locate these duties to God and the neighbour is the threefold-way of response to God's self-revelation. This way is portrayed in how Jesus, the true Israel(ite), responded to the Father. The people of Israel were summoned to walk in the way of the Lord who had led them from Egypt via Mount Sinai to the Land of Canaan. They were to fulfil their duties as the recipients of God's Law, as the adopted sons of God and as those whom God had chosen to have spiritual fellowship with. This is the threefold *Way* of Torah, Sonship and Knowledge. (There is a good exposition of this way by the Bishop John Tinsley in *The Imitation of God in Christ. An Essay on the Biblical Basis of Christian Spirituality*, London, 1960.)

The Old Testament informs us that the people of Israel failed in their covenant obligations and duties and did not walk after the Lord in his threefold way. But Jesus walked in this way perfectly, fulfilling all its duties: and he humbly claimed: 'I am the Way (because) I am the truth and the life' (John 14:6). Therefore, it is not surprising that the early Christians described what we now call Christianity as 'the Way' (Acts 9:2; 19:9; 19:23; 24:22).

11

Submitting to the Lord

In the Bible both male and female believers are called 'sons' of God. The reason for this is not merely the subordinate place women held in society. It is also that the attitude and duty of a son, especially a first-born son, in Jewish society is an admirable portrait of the relation of a believer to God, the Father.

FATHER AND SONS

Fatherhood included much more than begetting through sexual intercourse, followed by providing physical and material support as well as teaching a trade. It also involved showing and teaching the son the moral and spiritual way in which he ought to live and walk and guiding him along that way of life, the father himself providing a worthy example. The idea was that through obedient submission to the will of the father, the son becomes a perfect reproduction of his father at every point. So the advice of Solomon, often repeated in the Book of Proverbs is, 'My son, keep your father's commands' (6:20).

We find that the people of Israel are called the sons of God who are to imitate their Father and walk in his ways:

> You are the children of the Lord your God . . . Out of all the peoples on the face of the earth, the Lord has chosen you to be his treasured possession. (Deut 14:1–2)

> I will lead them [Israel] beside streams of water, on a level path where they will not stumble, because I am Israel's father, and Ephraim is my firstborn son. (Jer 31:9)

When Israel was a child, I loved him, and out of Egypt I called my son. But the more I called Israel, the further they went from me. (Hos 11:1)

As the last text reveals, Israel was more often a disobedient than obedient son, failing to keep the Father's commandments, and not walking in his ways.

Jesus, as the new Israel, succeeded where the old Israel had failed. We see in Jesus both a perfect submission to Joseph in Nazareth and a perfect submission to the Father in heaven. The Gospel of John has a particular interest in the latter and records Jesus saying:

My food is to do the will of him who sent me and to finish his work. (4:34)

For I have come down from heaven not to do my own will but to do the will of him who sent me. (6:38)

I have obeyed my Father's commands and remain in his love. (15:10)

The true Son is he who walks in the way of his Father, gladly submitted to his will. For Jesus, as we know, this meant the way of suffering, public death as a criminal and hurried burial in the grave of a stranger.

CHILDREN OF GOD

Christians are the children of God, adopted by the Father into his family, with Jesus as the elder Brother. Thus they pray, 'Our Father in heaven, hallowed be your name' (Matt 6:9). And as Paul explained:

When the time had fully come, God sent his Son, born of a woman, born under the law, to redeem those under the law, that we might receive the full rights of sons. Because you are sons, God sent the Spirit of his Son into our hearts, the Spirit who calls out, '*Abba*, Father'. (Gal 4:5–6)

Abba is the Aramaic word for 'Daddie' and used by offspring of all ages: Paul used it again when he wrote to the church in Rome. By the Spirit we cry, '*Abba*, Father', for 'the Spirit himself testifies with our spirit that we are God's children' (Rom 8:15).

As sons (children) of God we are duty-bound by gratitude and grace to submit wholeheartedly to the Father by obeying his will, which is revealed in and by Jesus Christ. What this means practically is written in every letter of the New Testament; but, let us keep to Galatians for from there we already have taken our primary text on Christians as the adopted sons of God. The quotations are all from chapter five.

1. On the principle that 'the sinful nature desires what is contrary to the Spirit, and the Spirit what is contrary to the sinful nature' (v.17) then (a) 'Do not use you freedom [in Christ from the guilt of sin] to indulge the sinful nature' (v.13); (b) 'Do not gratify the desires of the sinful nature' (v.16), and (c) 'Do not become conceited, provoking one another' (v.26).
2. 'Serve one another in love. The entire law is summed up in a single command, "Love your neighbour as yourself" ' (v.14).
3. 'Live [walk] by the Spirit' (v.16), 'be led by the Spirit' (v.18) and 'keep in step with the Spirit' (v.25).

Here we find three components of the submitted lives of God's children. First of all, their souls are filled with the Spirit of the Lord Jesus and he is the inspiration of their obedience. Because of his presence they produce the fruit of the Spirit – love, joy, peace, patience, kindness, goodness, faithfulness, gentleness and self-control (v.22). In the second place, they will obey the whole moral law of God as it concerns fellow human beings because they aim to love others after the example of Jesus. Thirdly, they positively reject sin, resist when tempted by Satan and put to death those desires arising from their [old] human nature which are contrary to the will of God.

Each of these three components can also be illustrated from the Letter to the Romans from which we also quoted Paul's teaching concerning Christians as sons of God. When we are constantly being filled with the Spirit then we are conscious of the Spirit helping us in our weakness. 'We do not know what we ought to pray, but the Spirit himself intercedes for us with groans that words cannot express. And he who searches our hearts knows the mind of the Spirit, because the Spirit intercedes for the saints in accordance with God's will' (8:26–27). Further, we are able to begin to love our neighbour because 'God has poured out his love into our hearts by the Holy Spirit, whom he has given us' (5:5; cf 13:8–10 and 15:11–4). Thirdly, as to the rejection of sinful thoughts, feelings and desires arising from the [old] sinful nature which we all possess (and will do so until we die) Paul has much to say.

Significantly, he says some of it in the centre of his great exposition of the ministry of the Spirit of the Lord Jesus in chapter eight. 'Those who live according to the sinful nature have their minds set on what that nature desires; but those who live in accordance with the Spirit have their minds set on what the Spirit desires' (8:5). However, since Christians have received the Holy Spirit to dwell in their hearts as the Spirit of Christ, they are under obligation to be submitted to Jesus and his Spirit. 'Therefore, we have an obligation – but it is not to the sinful nature, to live according to it. For if you live according to the sinful nature, you will die; but if you by the Spirit put to death the misdeeds of the body, you will live, because those who are led by the Spirit of God are sons of God' (8:13–14). Mortification is a slow, and sometimes painful process and experience (see further 6:11–15).

As we would expect from a long letter there is much more in Romans about the duty and joy of submission as sons to God the Father. There is submission to God as he works in his providence. 'We know that in all things God works for the good of those who love him, who have been called according to his purpose' (8:28). To live as a son means accepting what comes to us hour by hour as that which God has allowed or caused to happen to us so that in and through it we may learn to trust, love and serve him the more and better. And this includes pain and suffering: 'We also rejoice in our sufferings, because we know that suffering produces perseverance; perseverance character; and character hope' (5:4).

Then also there is submission to human government and laws through giving respect, honour, and obedience, as well as paying all rightful taxes (13:1–7). This is not done reluctantly, but gladly, for Christ's sake.

Finally, from this Letter we may note there is a submission one to another, and always in favour of the weaker sister and brother (chaps. 14–15). 'Make up your mind not to put any stumbling block or obstacle in your brother's way' (14:13). And 'Do not destroy the work of God for the sake of food. All food is clean, but it is wrong for a man to eat anything that causes someone else to stumble' (14:20). The corporate dimension is emphasised also by Paul in Ephesians 4–5. His summary is in 5:21: 'Submit to one another out of reverence for Christ.' This submission includes such things as earning money in order to share it with the fellowship and of speaking (at all times) for the good of others (4:28–32).

In the brief 1 John there is teaching on both the privileges and duties of children of God. First the joy and privilege of sonship:

> How great is the love the Father has lavished on us, that we should be called children of God: And that is what we are! The reason the world does not know us is that it did not know him. Dear friends, now are we the children of God, and what we will be has not yet been made known. But we know that when he appears we shall be like him, for we shall see him as he is. Everyone who has this hope in him purifies himself, just as he is pure. (3:1–3)

The joy and privilege lead to the duty of purification, the cleansing from moral stain through the resisting of all temptation to break the commands of God. And there are other duties of children of God:

> This is how we know who the children of God are and who the children of the devil are: Anyone who does not do what

is right is not a child of God: neither is anyone who does not love his brother. (3:10)

To do right (= to be righteous) is to keep God's commandments in heart and action. And the call to love the brother is again emphasised in verse 18. 'Dear children, let us not love with words or tongue [only] but with actions and in truth.' We all know that actions speak louder than words: and genuine actions (i.e. in truth) speak even louder.

To summarise. To be a child/son of God, and to belong to his adopted family with Christ as elder brother, is a great privilege bringing deep joy. It also means the duty of constant and unhesitant submission to God our Father. This submission is both in the keeping of his commandments and doing what is right and accepting without rebellion his providential government of our daily lives and affairs. We are gratefully and dutifully to respond to our Father with full mental persuasion, wholeheartedly and willingly.

12

Obeying the Lord

Torah is the name of the first five books of the Bible, the Books of Moses (Gen, Ex, Lev, Num, Deut). It means that which God has revealed for his children to believe and obey. Torah is all that God tells his covenant children of his own character, grace, mercy and faithfulness, as well as his statutes, ordinances, judgements, laws and commandments.

Torah is God's signpost pointing the way to follow him as the Lord.

Be careful to do what the Lord your God has commanded you: do not turn aside to the right or to the left. Walk in the way that the Lord your God has commanded you . . . (Deut 5:32)

Blessed are they whose ways are blameless,
who walk according to the law [Torah] of the Lord. (Ps 119:1)

He has shown you, O man, what is good. And what does the Lord require of you? To act justly, and to love mercy and to walk humbly with your God. (Micah 6:8)

The people of Israel were given Torah as God's revelation and gift to them. It was their duty to make it the foundation of their corporate and family and individual lives.

JESUS AND TORAH

Jesus saw the Torah as something both to be personally obeyed as a Jew within the old covenant and also to be brought to completion through his role and work as Messiah. This is why he gladly submitted to the baptism of John even though he had no sin to confess: 'Let it be so now; it is proper for us to do this to fulfil all righteousness' (Matt 3:15). And this is why he said: 'Do not think that I have come to abolish the Law [Torah] or the Prophets; I have not come to abolish them but to fulfil them' (Matt 5:17). And the fulfilment meant both bringing the revelation of God to its fulness and making the whole sacrificial system of the Temple obsolete through his sacrificial death at Calvary.

Jesus did not set aside the moral law contained in the Torah: he did not cancel the ten commandments (Ex 20). He said that the whole of the Torah as commandments from God could be summed up in two large commands. 'Love the Lord your God with all your heart and with all your soul and with all your mind and with all your strength', and 'Love your neighbour as yourself' (Mark 12:29–31). Love is to be that which controls both our interior and our exterior lives.

What loving God means in practice is seen in the example of Jesus. His ready and joyful submission to the will of the Father and his constant communion with him through trusting and obeying are to be placed alongside his using every opportunity for meditation, worship and prayer. What loving the neighbour means in practice is also seen in the example of Jesus. There is much food for thought in John 13. Here we read of the washing of the disciples sweaty and dusty feet by Jesus, of the protests of Peter, and the explanations of Jesus.

> You call me 'Teacher' and 'Lord' and rightly so, for that is what I am. Now that I, your Lord and Teacher, have washed your feet, you also should wash one another's feet. I have set you an example, that you should do as I have done for you. I tell you the truth, no servant is greater than his master, nor is a messenger greater than the one who sent him. Now

you know these things, you will be blessed if you do them. (13:13–17)

This is a dramatic illustration of self-giving love, that love contained in the new commandment: 'A new commandment I give you. Love one another. As I have loved you so you must love one another. All men will know that you are my disciples if you love one another' (13:34). But, we must always remember that such love in imitating Jesus is only possible because he first redeems his people – a theme which is clearly portrayed in his washing of the feet (13:10–11). A redeemed people are to love with Christ's love.

PAUL AND TORAH

When we turn to the teaching of Paul we find that he insists that Jesus Christ is the new Torah and, at the same time, the perfect example of obedience to the new Torah (1 Cor 9:20–21). As the fulness of the revelation of God to mankind, Jesus is the new Torah, the new signpost and way to the Father. His life, ministry, passion, sacrificial death and glorious resurrection, along with his teaching concerning the kingdom of God and his own role and identity, constitute God's revelation. By looking to Jesus, studying him and his teaching, we see both what God is like and what God requires. Christ as the eternal Son of God in human flesh is the new Torah. 'Christ is the end of the law' (Rom 10:4), meaning that Christ is the embodiment and the completion of Torah.

The example of Jesus as well as his teaching, says Paul, is love. The Son of God 'loved me and gave himself for me' (Gal 2:20) and his love 'compels us' (2 Cor 5:14) to seek to imitate him. The entire law with regard to our obligations to other people is summed up in the single command to love your neighbour as yourself (Gal 5:14; Rom 13:8–10). In fact the only thing that counts, says Paul, 'is faith expressing itself through love' (Gal 5:6) and this applies equally to both Jew and Gentile. And what love means in practice is beautifully and movingly portrayed in the hymn of love found in 1 Corinthians 13. Love is an interior virtue which must express itself externally in attitude, word and behaviour:

> Love is patient, love is kind. It does not envy, it does not boast, it is not proud. It is not rude, it is not self-seeking, it is not easily angered, it keeps no record of wrongs. Love does not delight in evil but rejoices with the truth.

Such love is the gift of God through the presence of the Spirit of the Lord Jesus Christ (wonderfully explained in Rom 5:1–5). But it is also the result of continued prayer, of definite putting to death of sinful and selfish desires (Rom 8:13; 13:14; Gal 6:7–10), and of a conscious attempt to imitate Jesus.

But let us take another look at these words from 1 Corinthians 13. It is as if Paul has passed love as a beam of light through a crystal prism and it has come out of the other side broken up into its component colours – red and blue, and all the other colours of the rainbow. Love has nine ingredients – patience, kindness, humility, courtesy, unselfishness, calmness (good temper), guilelessness and sincerity. All these relate to attitudes and actions towards other people.

Patience. 'Love is patient.' Love is calm and not in a hurry; but is always ready to do its work when the call is heard or felt. In the meantime, it is being expressed as a meek and quiet spirit.

Kindness. 'Love is kind.' Jesus spent a lot of his time doing kind things to and for people. Love is expressed in a sympathetic and friendly nature, always ready to help where help is needed.

Generosity. 'Love does not envy.' Love does not know the feeling of ill-will towards anybody; it is always magnanimous and will never put anyone down.

Humility. 'Love does not boast and is not proud.' Love relinquishes the right of self-congratulation and self-satisfaction. It puts a seal on the lips and causes the mind to forget what has been done for others.

Courtesy. 'Love is not rude.' This is love in relation to etiquette: it is politeness in society; it is gracious behaviour in company.

Unselfishness. 'Love is not self-seeking.' Love knows that the greatest happiness is in giving, not only of goods but of time, energy, and commitment. It is not seeking things for ourselves but always wanting the best for others.

Calmness. 'Love is not easily angered.' There is no place or even possibility for a quick temper or touchy disposition where love reigns.

Guilelessness. 'Love keeps no record of wrongs.' Love is not suspicious and does not remember faults in order to use them to put down a person. Love sees the bright side and puts the best construction on every action.

Sincerity. 'Love does not delight in evil but rejoices with the truth.' Here love is the self-restraint which refuses to make capital out of the faults of others; it delights in not exposing the weaknesses of others but in seeking to understand them; it is the sincerity of purpose which tries to see things as they are and rejoices to find them better than suspicion feared or slander denounced.

Love is not an emotion; it is a movement of the will, inspired by heart and mind. Love is a rich, strong, manly, vigorous expression of the truly Christian character. And it is a character which is built up by ceaseless practice. As Jesus himself increased in wisdom and favour with God and man (Luke 2:52) and as he learned obedience through daily experience (Heb 5:8) so the character of love, with its constituent parts, is built up (by the grace of God) through practice. Each day provides opportunities for the exercise of most if not all the ingredients of love: these have to be taken and used to allow the love of God to flow through us. Yet we are to be more than channels of the love of God. We are to be reservoirs from which channels flow. The love of God is to fill our hearts/minds as a reservoir so that as occasion demands that love can flow in the appropriate channel of attitude/activity to our fellow human beings.

But what about the ten commandments? Did Paul think there was no need to obey them? The answer is that Paul believed that in truly loving God after the example of Jesus's love of the Father we shall truly only worship the One God who is the Lord, we shall place no idol before us to bow down to it, we shall not misuse the holy name of God, and we shall remember the Sabbath (by remembering the new Sabbath). Further, in loving the neighbour after the example of Jesus's love for his fellow men, we shall honour our parents, not commit murder or adultery, not steal or give false witness and not covet what belongs to others. Further, because love of God and fellow creatures begins in the heart we shall obey these commandments not only externally but also internally – not committing adultery or murder, for example, in intention and desire.

If we seek to obey the commandments in and by our own strength and according to our own interpretations then we find we are forever feeling guilty and powerless. It is important to read carefully the seventh chapter of the Letter to the church in Rome to gain insight in this area of spirituality. Only with the aim of loving God and neighbour after the example of Christ and in his strength as a forgiven child of God will we fulfil the moral law of God.

JOHN AND TORAH

It will be profitable now to turn to the inspired wisdom of the apostle John in his first Letter. For him love is the fulfilment of the moral law and he writes:

> This is how we know what love is: Jesus Christ laid down his life for us. And we ought to lay down our lives for our brothers. If anyone has material possessions and sees his brother in need but has no pity on him, how can the love of God be in him? Dear children, let us not love with words or tongue but with actions and in truth . . . (3:16–18)

Love not only goes out into action for the good of others it also drives fear from our hearts – 'perfect love drives out fear, because fear has to do with punishment' (4:18). Further, the love of God for us and in us means we have to be discriminating in what we love:

> Do not love the world or anything in the world. If anyone loves the world, the love of the Father is not in him. For everything in the world – the cravings of sinful man, the lust of his eyes and the boasting of what he has and does – comes not from the Father but from the world. The world and its desires pass away, but the man who does the will of God lives for ever. (2:15–17)

The 'world' has various meanings. It can mean the physical universe or 'the human race living on the earth'. Here it is neither of these. It is an inclusive term for all those people who are in the kingdom of darkness and have not been born of God. It is people as they are influenced by Satan, sin and evil. The command not to love this world is based on two arguments – the incompatibility of loving both the Father and this world; and the transience of this world as compared with the eternity of those who are in Christ and do God's will. For if a person is engrossed in both the outlook and pursuits of those who reject the love of God in Jesus Christ, it is evident that she/he cannot genuinely love the Father. This teaching has all kinds of ramifications in everyday life.

To summarise. Jesus Christ has fulfilled the old Torah and in so doing become in himself the new Torah. To us he is also the example *par excellence* of obedience to Torah. Such obedience is summarised in one word, love. The new covenant, inaugurated by the bloody, sacrificial death of Jesus on the Cross, binds Christian believers to love God and each other (together with all neighbours) in imitation of the love of Jesus. This duty to love never changes.

13

Knowing the Lord

The Hebrew language has all kinds of interesting features. But in one particular it is unique. It uses the verb 'to know' of sexual intercourse and because of this 'to know' can sometimes point to deep, personal and intimate relationships where no sexual overtones are involved. It can also be used in the same way as the verb is used in ordinary English – to know about things or people.

THE OLD TESTAMENT

So when we read that God has chosen the people of Israel and that he knows them, we understand this to refer to a special, covenant relationship which he has with them. 'You only have I *known* of all the families of the earth' (Amos 3:1, RV; NIV paraphrases using 'chosen'). Likewise when Israel is called upon to know God, or is chastised by the prophets for failing to know God, we understand this to refer to a failure to trust, worship, love and serve him. ' "Let him who boasts boast about this: that he understands and *knows* me, that I am the Lord, who exercises kindness, justice and righteousness on earth, for in these I delight" declares the Lord' (Jer 9:24). And referring to a king now dead, Jeremiah also declared as God's mouthpiece: ' "He defended the cause of the poor and needy, and so all went well. Is that not what it means to know me?" declares the Lord' (22:16). A right relationship with God leads to a right concern for deprived people.

The Old Testament is the account of the Lord who always *knows* his people and of these people often failing to *know* the

96

Lord. However, one of the characteristics of the future Messiah in the prophecies of the Old Testament is that he will be known of God and truly know him (Is 11:2,9; 53:11); and through this knowledge he will bring salvation to the people. Jesus is presented in the Gospels as the One who truly knows the Father even as the Father knows the Son. Jesus said: 'All things have been committed to me by my Father. No-one knows the Son except the Father, and no-one knows the Father except the Son and those to whom the Son chooses to reveal him' (Matt 11:27; cf Lk 10:22).

JOHN'S GOSPEL

This intimate relationship of love between Father and Son is especially emphasised in the Gospel of John. Speaking to the Jews about his relationship to the Father, Jesus said: 'Though you do not know him, I know him. If I said I did not, I would be a liar like you, but I do know him and keep his word' (8:55). And speaking of his relationship to his true disciples Jesus said: 'I am the good shepherd; I know my sheep and my sheep know me – just as the Father knows me and I know the Father – and I lay down my life for the sheep' (10:14–15). Here an intimate relationship leads to a costly action. In his great prayer before his arrest Jesus said: 'Righteous Father, though the world does not know you, I know you, and they [the disciples] know that you have sent me. I have made you known to them, and they will continue to make you known in order that the love you have for me may be in them and that I myself may be in them' (17:25–26). Knowledge is expressed in love, the deep and intimate love of God for himself, and for his children.

So we see that knowledge is not merely having information about God and Christ, it is being in such a close relationship with the Godhead that the love which is of the essence of the Godhead flows into the believer and through him to the world. Do not Satan and all the evil angels know all about God and his ways? Yet they do not love him, worship him or obey him. The knowledge of God which Jesus has and which he shares with his disciples is a knowledge that is an intimate relationship, leading to loving worship, obedience and service.

PAUL'S LETTERS

In the Letters of Paul we find that the verb 'to know' and the noun 'knowledge' are often used in their ordinary meanings. For example, possession of information or facts about Christianity can be dangerous, says Paul. 'Knowledge puffs up' but, in contrast, 'love builds up' (1 Cor 8:1ff). And he adds, 'So this weak brother, for whom Christ died, is destroyed by your knowledge' (v. 11). Here knowledge leads to pride, vanity, lack of care and sin.

'Knowing' is also used, as we would expect of one who was 'a Hebrew of the Hebrews', of an intimate relationship between God and those who believe and trust in his Son. At the end of the great hymn of love in 1 Corinthians 13, Paul wrote this: 'Now we see but a poor reflection; then [in the kingdom of God] we shall see face to face. Now I know in part; then I shall know fully, even as I am fully known [now by the Lord Jesus].' And addressing the Galatian churches he reminded them of their former pagan position and what God had done for them in Christ by the Holy Spirit. 'Formerly when you did not know God, you were slaves to those who by nature are not gods. But now that you know God – or rather are known by God – how is it that you are turning back to those weak and miserable principles?' (4:8–9). Here he reflects his conviction that the believer only knows [is in intimate fellowship with] God because God has taken the initiative in knowing [regenerating and causing his Spirit to dwell within] him.

Of course, it would be wrong to separate this knowing which is spiritual union with God from that knowing about God, his character, his gospel, his promises and his kingdom. Those who know God intimately as Father must also have a minimum doctrinal and ethical knowledge about God and his revelation. And the greater is their knowledge of God's revelation and will, and the greater their understanding of Christ, his identity, mission and glory, then also the greater is the possibility (in the right spiritual framework) of a deeper knowledge of God in terms of communion and fellowship. However, knowledge about the Bible, theology, ethics, church history and worship does not of itself guarantee spiritual fellowship with God.

The ideal situation is where there is a growth in knowledge about God, Christ and the Holy Spirit and this is matched by a deepening relationship of love and trust in God. Then we are known by God and we truly know him. In fact, each Christian has put on in conversion 'the new self, which is being renewed in knowledge in the image of its Creator' (Col 3:10) when he lives as a Christian ought to live. And to live as we ought to do our minds need to be constantly renewed by the Holy Spirit. Paul emphasises this throughout his Letters, and nowhere more strongly than in that to the Ephesians. Here is one of his prayers:

> I keep asking that the God of our Lord Jesus Christ, the glorious Father, may give you the Spirit of wisdom and revelation so that you may know him better. I pray also that the eyes of your heart may be enlightened in order that you may know the hope to which he has called you . . . (1:17–18)

The renewal of the mind is certainly the work of the Holy Spirit; but, it is also achieved by the Holy Spirit as we fulfil our duties of meditation and prayer. We must both hear Scripture read in church and read Scripture privately in order to become familiar with God's revelation, especially his self-disclosure in Jesus Christ. We must hear sermons on that revelation and we must make time to meditate (consider, reflect upon, apply to our own lives) this revelation. Further this hearing and this meditating are to be turned to prayer, asking God to help us grow morally and spiritually according to the light we have gained from his Word.

Paul often calls upon his readers to engage in meditation and consideration. He urged the Philippians to consider the humility of Jesus, incarnate Son, who humbled himself even to death on a cross, and to imitate his holy example (2:5ff). He told the Colossians to raise their minds to think of Jesus in glory: 'Since, then, you have been raised with Christ, set your heart on things

above, where Christ is seated at the right hand of God. Set
your minds on things above, not on earthly things' (3:1–2).
And he advises the Ephesians to consider the armour of the
Roman soldier as a way of recognising what spiritual armour
God has provided for his 'soldiers' as they are attacked by
Satan and evil powers (6:10ff).

As to prayer, we notice that Paul's Letters contain many
prayers. Thinking of his converts and their needs he often
breaks into prayer. Also he urged all believers to constant
prayer: 'Be joyful always; pray continually; give thanks in all
circumstances, for this is God's will for you in Christ Jesus' (1
Thess 5:17). He did not mean that we are to do nothing else
but pray for how can we pray if we are engaged in some
necessary, absorbing activity like serving a customer or answering the questions of an insistent child? He meant that we are
to turn to prayer often throughout the day – to perhaps longer
prayer on waking and retiring and shorter prayers as occasion
arises and circumstances permit. Hereby we shall keep God
constantly in mind, be aware of his presence, and seek his
guidance and blessing on the day's events and circumstances.
Continual prayer also means regular prayer day by day as well
as through each day. Here we may recall that both Jesus and
Paul were brought up to use the Psalter as their book of
prayers, to learn the psalms and to pray them as prayers for
themselves and/or for their people, Israel. Over the centuries
the Church has followed this practice and many people have
prayed – and continue to pray – the psalms as personal prayers
day by day, month by month, year by year.

I JOHN

There is much food for thought concerning knowledge in 1
John. In the opening paragraph John tells us that 'our fellowship is with the Father and with his Son, Jesus Christ' (1:3) and
a little later he explains:

> We know that we have come to know him [Jesus Christ] if
> we obey his commands. The man who says, 'I know him'

but does not do what he commands is a liar, and the truth
is not in him. But if anyone obeys his word, God's love is
truly made complete in him. This is how we know we are in
him: Whoever claims to live in him must walk as Jesus did.
(2:3–6)

Here the verb 'to know' is used in the general sense, 'we know
that', and in the Hebrew sense, 'to know him'. The knowledge
of intimate fellowship has the direct implication, says John, of
obedience and imitating the Lord Jesus.

At the end of the short Letter there is this paragraph:

We know that anyone born of God does not continue to sin;
[Jesus Christ] the one who was born of God keeps him safe,
and the evil one does not touch him. We know that we are
children of God and that the whole world is under the control
of the evil one. We also know that the Son of God has come
and has given us understanding, so that we may know him
who is true. And we are in him who is true – even in his Son
Jesus Christ. He is the true God and eternal life.(5:18–20)

Here the 'we know' is not human confidence alone: it is a
humble confidence arising from the inner prompting of the
Holy Spirit. It exists because 'we' are in a relationship with
God in which he treats us as his dear children. And not only
are we protected from the sinister power of Satan; we also
habitually and decidedly do not intend to commit sin. That is,
we do not desire and attempt ever to break the commandments
of God, especially the command to love one another. However,
when we do fall and fail we look to God the Father through
the Lord Jesus: 'If we confess our sins, he is faithful and just
and will forgive us our sins and purify us from all unrighteous-
ness' (1:9).

To summarise. Knowing God is only possible when we are
known by God as our Father. While such knowing is always a
personal relationship and thus deeper than intellectual knowledge about it, it normally also includes knowledge about the
Lord, Father, Son and Holy Spirit – his character, his way and

his will. The apostolic Letters of the New Testament emphasise the necessity of receiving and believing sound doctrine in mind and heart: and the apostles oppose error and heresy in most of their Letters. The need to receive sound doctrine today includes the duty of studying the Bible to learn of God and his ways and also of learning and studying the Creeds (Apostles', Nicene and Athanasian) as summaries of Christian doctrine.

The same Letters also emphasise that being in communion with God, and ever longing for deeper, richer communion, is of the essence of the new covenant. They expound the prophecy of Jeremiah concerning the new covenant: 'This is the covenant that I will make . . . I will put my law in their minds and write it on their hearts. I will be their God and they shall be my people. No longer will a man teach his neighbour or a man his brother, saying "Know the Lord", because they will all *know* me from the least of them to the greatest . . .' (31:31ff; cf Heb 10:15–16). And because knowledge is personal relationship the apostles insist upon all those duties which increase such knowledge, particularly corporate worship and prayer. Included in the former is fellowship with believers, the ministry of word and sacrament: included in the latter is meditation, adoration, praise, thanksgiving, confession of sin, petition and intercession.

Spirituality must include the duties of study, prayer and corporate worship.

PART FOUR

Choosing the Way

14

Examining my Faith

We have arrived at the point in our investigation where we must begin to look into our own hearts and minds. It is possible – alas! – to reduce even the most practical of topics into merely an intellectual or cerebral exercise. For example, there are courses in spirituality in theological colleges/seminaries where the students are examined in their proficiency in exactly the same way as in a course in sociology or history. Whether or not the study has become food for their souls in relationship to God is of no importance as far as completing the course is concerned.

The same type of thing happens outside places of academic learning. You or I can become an expert in spirituality without being wholeheartedly committed to communion with God. We can devour books, discuss concepts and disciplines, and speak of prayer without our interior lives being touched by the grace of God.

Therefore, each of us must sincerely and earnestly ask: Is spirituality for me?

That is, is it for me who am God's creature, sinful but yet still made in his image, after his likeness? For me – a sinner for whom the incarnate Son of God suffered and died?

Before proceeding with this question it will perhaps sharpen the focus if we recall, as succinctly as possible, the substance of our exposition of spirituality in Parts One to Three.

WHAT IS SPIRITUALITY?

Spirituality is following in the way of the Holy Spirit, who is the Spirit of Christ to those who believe. Its motivation is simply expressed in the reaching for the Ideal and aiming for the Goal. These are presented in Scripture terms of 'Be perfect, be holy and be righteous' as God himself is perfect, holy and righteous. The way of the Spirit of Christ for Christians is to be perfect, holy and righteous to the fullest extent that forgiven creatures can possibly be so both in this life (in weak, mortal bodies) and in the resurrection life (in immortal, glorious bodies). What is reached for, and aimed at, in this life can also be expressed as: 'Be godly, pious, devoted and religious.' In one phrase the aim is 'to be like Jesus'.

Spirituality is also using the means supplied by, and doing the duties urged by, the Spirit of Christ, as the route into the Ideal and path to the Goal. These include wholehearted participation in Christian fellowship and worship (the ministry of word and sacrament), along with daily trusting in the promises, readily submitting to the will, and happily obeying the commands of the Lord Jesus.

Spirituality is a personal response to the God of all grace: but, it is not to be individualistic. It is a personal response within a community response: and the community is the Church of Christ.

But to what extent – if at all – is spirituality a political, economic and social programme?

In his *God of Surprises* Gerard Hughes SJ presents commitment to immediate nuclear disarmament as a necessary outcome of his spirituality. Kenneth Leech in his *True God. An exploration in spiritual theology* goes much further and advocates social and political involvement of a socialist kind as a necessary part of any true spirituality.

My response to these influential writers (and others who incorporate particular social, political and economic views in their definition of spirituality) is, in brief, the following. I want to insist, first of all, that spirituality must include (or lead to) the loving of the neighbour as a person made in God's image as well as the duty of witnessing always and everywhere for

Christ. But the precise ways in which this loving and witnessing are done takes us out of spirituality into other areas – ethics, evangelism, mission and so on. Spirituality relates more to the preparation and motivation of the Church and individual Christian for active service with mind, heart, will and body than to the details of actual service for the kingdom.

As there are different types of spirituality so there are different ways of expressing the love of Christ in the spheres of evangelism, mission and ethics as well as politics. Contexts in which people live are different (e.g. a Marxist, Islamic and secular Western State) and these demand different approaches. Further, since politics relates to the art of the possible even the choicest of saints have had, do have and will have different views as to what is right, most effective for the kingdom of God and achievable in any given situation. If we tie spirituality to a specific view of politics, economics and social theory then we go too far.

Having said this, I do think that we need to insist on two points: first, that a human being is to be seen as a unity of body and soul and ought therefore to experience harmony between the interior and exterior aspects of the one life. Thus an interior spirituality of communion with God ought to be united to an exterior life of loving service of God and fellow human beings (which service can of course take many different forms). And, secondly, that a human being must be seen within her/his life context and not as a soul without a body and without a life in community. Thus spirituality has to become practical within the real life situation.

It seems to me that a right appreciation of the Christian life in terms of the *imitatio Christi*, the imitation of Jesus who loved God and his fellow human beings, helps to unite the interior and exterior aspects of the Christian life and to view the context in which that life has to be lived. As the outcome of his communion with, and obedience of the Father, Jesus actually involved himself lovingly and unsparingly in the lives of those whom he helped.

The imitation of Jesus does not mean seeking to be a Messiah. It relates to studying and copying him in terms of his faith, trust, love, obedience in relation to the Father, his

humility and compassion in relation to humanity, and his practical readiness to put himself out and to go the extra mile on
behalf of the needy. Such a spirituality knows no dichotomy
between soul and body and seeks to view a person or people
in their real context.

Such imitation is the true following of Jesus and can only be
generated in the heart through sincere and prayerful reading
of the Gospels so that the example of Jesus, as well as his
teaching, is imprinted in the mind and desired as the ideal by
the heart. Today much of our reading is to gain information
and so we skim over the page and do not absorb the content.
Meditational reading, which is necessary to begin the life of
imitating Jesus, has to be slow, prayerful and formational: it is
a different method and approach to that which we normally
use in everyday activity.

If, by the cultivation of this method, we are able to move
towards the uniting of the interior and exterior aspects of spirituality, we ought not to make political, social and economic
theories/positions a part of a definition of spirituality. It is quite
wrong to claim that to have a right relationship with God you
must be an active socialist; and it is just as wrong to claim that
God only approves of supporting capitalism. Spirituality may be
compared to lighting a fire and keeping it alight and providing
warmth – who and what it warms are important but we can
separate them from the fire itself. Or it may be compared to
planting a garden and tending it – who come to see it and
where the flowers from it are taken are important but we can
separate these from the garden itself. However, the fire is
intended to give light and heat, and a garden is meant to
produce beautiful sights and scents. So spirituality is not merely
the cultivation of a relationship with God: it is the loving of
God and the neighbour in practical ways.

FAITH AND GROWTH

I recognise that the question, 'Is spirituality for me?' is rarely
asked in this particular form. Further, it is only asked when a
person has been a Christian for a while and becomes aware

that there is much more to 'believing in Jesus' than at first appeared; further it is asked when there is a longing in the heart to draw closer to God. In fact true believing, real saving faith, is the key which unlocks a heavenly gate: rays of divine sunshine flood the soul and hearty desires to be more deeply immersed in the love of God are aroused.

From the human standpoint faith lies at the very centre of being a Christian: and faith is intended to grow and keep on growing, as the soul takes a more firm grip upon God's promises of grace. Paul told the church in Corinth that 'our hope is that, as your faith continues to grow, our area of activity among you will greatly expand' (2 Cor 10:15). He wanted their cooperation so that he could preach the gospel in the regions beyond their city (v.16). Writing to the church to the north of Corinth in Thessalonica he said: 'We ought always to thank God for you, brothers, and rightly so, because your faith is growing more and more . . .' (2 Thess 1:3).

Faith as the believing of certain facts which are entirely and wholly trustworthy – for example concerning the Incarnation of the Son of God, his ministry, suffering, death and exaltation – will certainly increase through the learning process within Christian fellowship and through personal reading and meditation upon the Scriptures. I've been studying the Bible and theology for over twenty years and I learn something new each week to strengthen and buttress my believing in Jesus Christ. There really is no limit to growth in understanding of God's revelation to us, in and through Jesus Christ.

Faith as the trusting of God through Jesus Christ and embracing wholeheartedly his promises, precepts, counsels and commands as the Word of God, for me also grows as it is nourished through meditation, prayer, worship and practically doing the will of God day by day.

However, it would be misleading to suggest that faith is always a simple, steady growth. It can be severely tested by temptation and periods of doubt and darkness. Here faith clings on to the promises of God even as a person thrown overboard clings to a piece of floating timber. Yet there are also moments of intense illumination of heart/mind when a profound experience of the presence of God makes everything seem so simple and overwhelmingly real. Then to believe in heaven and its glories seems as natural as – in ordinary life – believing that as we travel on the road we walk on firm ground. When the mind seems to descend into the heart and when intellect and feelings are simultaneously and firmly fixed upon Jesus then faith appears to be the most appropriate response of the soul to God. 'I know whom I have believed and I am convinced that he is able to guard what I have entrusted to him for that [final] day' (2 Tim 1:12).

As the infant grows into the child and on into the adult, so the 'new creation' (Gal 6:15) implanted in the believing soul by the Spirit of the Lord Jesus in regeneration/conversion is to grow within and through us. Regrettably this growth can be prevented or stunted through the resistance we offer via our pride, selfishness and tendency to please the world rather than the living God. As the sphere of influence of the Spirit of Christ within the believer increases so she/he grows in faith, as we have seen.

Closely related to the growth in believing and trusting is the growth in loving, for, as Paul taught, 'faith expresses itself through love' (Gal 5:6). In fact Paul prayed that his converts would love one another: 'May the Lord make your love increase and overflow for each other and for everyone else, just as ours does for you' (1 Thess 3:12). By the time he wrote his second Letter to Thessalonica the apostle could thank God for their loving one another: 'We ought always to thank God . . . because the love every one of you has for each other is increasing' (2 Thess 1:3).

Paul also prayed and looked for a growth in both good works (as the fruit of genuine faith) and in knowledge of God. 'We pray that you may live a life worthy of the Lord and may please him in every way: bearing fruit in every good work, growing in the knowledge of God, being strengthened with all power according to his glorious might . . .' (Col 1:10). Concerning the fruit of good works, Paul said this to the Corinthians: 'Now God who supplies seed to the sower and bread for food will also supply and increase your store of seed and will enlarge the harvest of your righteousness' (2 Cor 9:10). And Peter connected growing in the grace of God with growing in knowledge of God – for knowledge is both communion with God as well as knowing what he is like, what he has done, what he does and what he will do. 'But grow in the grace and knowledge of our Lord and Saviour Jesus Christ' (2 Pet 3:18).

So questions that I need to ask myself are such as these: Am I growing in the grace and knowledge of the Lord Jesus? Is my faith increasing in terms of trusting God and believing truths concerning him? Do I produce a growing harvest of good deeds for my fellow human beings as I seek to love them?

We said earlier that spirituality is personal but not individualistic. Growth is certainly personal but it is not individualistic. For my growing in faith, love, knowledge and producing the harvest of righteousness can only continue in so far as I am part of a worshipping fellowship of believers who are also growing together. If my hand grows faster than my arm then the result looks and feels odd. If one leg grows faster than the other then I cannot walk straight. Likewise true growth has not only to be in all the graces and virtues within the individual Christians but also as part of the general growth of Christian society.

Paul emphasises this growth in his Letters to Colossae and Ephesus. He told the Colossians that Christ is the Head and Lifegiver of the Church and from him 'the whole body, supported and held together by its ligaments and sinews, grows as God causes it to grow' (Col 2:19). Certainly the growth of the Church in true spirituality is caused by the presence and power of the Holy Spirit: but it only occurs where there is a fellowship of expectant, trusting and obedient Christians. 'In Christ Jesus the whole building is joined together and rises to become a holy temple in the Lord. And in him you are being built together to become a dwelling in which God lives by his Spirit' he told the Ephesians (2:21–22). And he also said that 'speaking the truth in love, we will in all things grow up into him who is the Head, that is, Christ' (Eph 4:15).

So, together with the personal examination of my faith, I need to ask questions as to whether the local church to which I belong is also growing into Christ, the Head, in faith, knowledge, love and fruit of righteousness. Here, of course, I must be exceedingly careful not to judge my fellow believers but to ask these questions in such a way that they become part of my duty to love my fellow Christians.

Christian spirituality is, therefore, certainly for me if I have begun the Christian life and feel the need to grow in faith, knowledge and love towards maturity, in the fellowship of others who also want to grow.

The examination of my soul and my decision to act upon the results of that examination do not occur in a moral and spiritual vacuum. God addresses me where I am and I hear him with my inward ears in my circumstances.

In the rest of Part Four we shall look at the contrasting religious contexts in which those, who want to draw near to God, hear and feel the call to examine themselves and choose to be like Jesus. We shall also reflect a little on the differences in human personality which affect to some degree how we respond. Finally I shall be very practical and urge a serious commitment through the entering into a personal covenant with the Lord.

15

Unity in Essentials

If you intend to travel by train or road from London to Scotland you must choose between an eastern route via Yorkshire or a western route via Lancashire. Christianity spirituality, likewise, does not exist as one route and one route only: there are several, perhaps even many, valid expressions of it.

Travelling by road you need a motor vehicle. Cars come in a variety of sizes, models and specifications; however, it is often the case that groups of outwardly different cars possess the same engine and gearbox, despite the variety of colours and styling and number of doors. We may say that the differing expressions of authentic Christian spirituality are, likewise, powered by the same unit – the presence and power of the Spirit of Christ, producing holiness and righteousness; and they are all heading for the same goal, even if apparently by different routes.

BROAD TYPES

It is very obvious that there are definite differences between Roman Catholic and Protestant expressions of Christian spirituality. Roman Catholics will pray not only to God the Father through Jesus Christ but also to Mary, the Mother of Jesus, and to the saints. They will confess their sins not only to God himself in the name of Jesus Christ but also to the priest whom they believe acts in God's stead. They will attempt to go to Mass several times a week, daily if possible, and will offer prayers both for the living and the dead. And in examining their consciences they will make a distinction between venial and mortal sins.

In contrast, Protestants will go in search of a sound ministry of the Word, where the preacher faithfully expounds the teaching of Holy Scripture. They will read their Bibles daily, exercising the right of private judgement, and praying only to God the Father in the name of the Lord Jesus. They will see the need not only for public worship on the Lord's Day but also for mid-week meetings for prayer and corporate bible-study. And they will insist that we are saved by faith, and by faith alone, but this is to be expressed in good works.

Yet if we take long enough to compare the two systems which have been called sacramental and prophetic in nature, we shall find that they have more in common than in difference. For example, take the content of the Creeds – Nicene and Apostles'. The Roman Catholic and Protestant expressions of Christian spirituality are solidly based on these confessions of the one Faith. They are trinitarian and teach that we come to God through, with and in the Incarnate Son of God. Further, they share the same Ideal and Goal – the beatific vision of the glory of God in the face of Jesus Christ in heaven.

Each system has produced 'saints' and yet each system can degenerate into both a mere nominal form of Christianity and a warped expression of religion. From each side people, who are genuinely desirous of being holy and righteous, nevertheless feel that the other side teaches and supports erroneous and false views of God and his grace. What most bothers the Protestant is the place of Mary and the saints in Roman Catholic devotion and what most bothers the Roman Catholic is the place of private judgement in Protestant Bible Study.

If we add for purposes of comparison the expression of spirituality in the Orthodox Churches of Greece and Russia we encounter yet further differences of emphasis, which are strange both to Roman Catholics as well as Protestants – for example the place of icons in worship and private prayers.

Not only are there broad types of spirituality within Christianity, there are also subdivisions within the broad types. These differences relate to the means and methods of spirituality. Within Roman Catholicism there are differences between the Cistercian, Franciscan, Carmelite, Jesuit and Dominican forms of spirituality as there are also differences between those who maintain old, well-tried methods and those who experiment with new methods of prayer, meditation, confession of sins and retreats. Further there are differences between those who claim that spirituality is to be used of our response to God in heart, attitude and word (but leaving to subjects like ethics the wider circle of social and political involvement) and those who want to say that a spirituality, which does not lead a person to direct involvement in the search for justice and peace in God's world, is a false spirituality. Gerard W. Hughes SJ claims too much in saying that 'any spirituality which cocoons us from the pain of this world, or which declares that the Church should keep out of politics and social justice questions, is a false spirituality and an idolatry' (*God of Surprises*, epilogue).

What is true of Roman Catholicism is even more true of Protestantism. Each basic tradition (and subdivision of a tradition) has its own particular emphases which produce a distinctive expression of spirituality. Some expressions are confined within a denomination while others are inter-denominational and they come (especially in America) in a bewildering variety – as watching TV stations on Sunday mornings quickly reveals. To examine them all would require not only a book but several books. Here we shall describe in brief only three. If you wish to look at others I commend *Protestant Spiritual Traditions* (ed. Frank C. Senn, Mahwah, NJ, 1986).

THE METHODIST WAY

First of all *Methodism* as it is portrayed in the writings of John and hymns of Charles Wesley as well as in the practice of the first fifty or so years of its existence. I shall use the first person singular in my description.

Aim/Goal of spirituality. The aim I have been taught is for my heart and soul to be filled with the love of God so that I maintain a state of perfect love to God and my neighbour.

O Love divine, how sweet thou art!
When shall I find my willing heart
   All taken up by Thee?
I thirst, I faint, I die to prove
The greatness of redeeming love,
   The love of Christ for me.

I feel I must pray like this:

O grant that nothing in my soul
May dwell, but thy pure love alone!
O may thy love possess me whole,
My joy, my treasure and my crown;
Strange fires far from my heart remove;
My every act, word, thought, be love!

To love God perfectly, as he deserves, is to be the very aim of
all my existence.

Ways and Means of spirituality. God has given me free-will to
respond to his riches of grace offered me in the gospel concerning the Lord Jesus Christ. I freely and gladly choose Jesus: I
turned from my sin and embraced Jesus my Saviour after I
heard a powerful sermon from a Methodist evangelist. With
tears in my eyes I believed in the name of the Son of God,
who has delivered me from the wrath to come and won for me
the forgiveness of my sins. And having made this turning to
Christ I testified of it to my family and neighbours.

Then I joined the local society of Methodists who met one
evening each week. Here I learned what Christian fellowship
really means.

All praise to our redeeming Lord,
   Who joins us by His grace,
And bids us, each to each restored,
   Together seek His face.
He bids us build each other up;
   And, gathered into one.
To our high calling's glorious hope,
   We hand in hand go on.

Here I was taught how to read and meditate upon the Bible, pray to God in praise and petition, thanksgiving and intercession. Here I was taught (and continue to be taught) how to witness for Jesus at home and work, and how to meet hostility and difficulty. Here I am always encouraged to make full use of the means of grace available in public worship in church, in the administration of Holy Communion and the ministry of the preaching of the Word.

Each week I go to the society meeting (the class meeting) and with a dozen or so others I share how the Lord has been leading me during the past week and how I have responded. We rejoice together, we help each other, we pray for one another, we sing together and exhort one another to be faithful to Jesus day by day. Our leader helps me personally where I have specific questions or difficulties.

Each morning I seek to arise early from my bed and have time to read my Bible and pray before going off to work. I want to go out as a servant of my Lord.

Forth in thy name, O Lord, I go,
  My daily labour to pursue,
Thee, only Thee, resolved to know
  In all I think, or speak, or do.

The task Thy wisdom hath assigned
  O let me cheerfully fulfil,
In all my works Thy presence find,
  And prove Thy acceptable will.

And at the end of the day I examine my conscience before the Lord, asking for forgiveness, giving thanks, praying for those with whom I have had contact and committing the night into his care and keeping.

I seek to live by faith each day, trusting in the merits of my Saviour; I look to him to give me the assurance of his Spirit in my heart so that I can feel the Spirit witnessing with my spirit that I am a child of God. Every opportunity to do good for others or to tell them of the love of Jesus I hope to use for the glory of my God. And in and through all this I pray God to fill my soul with his love so that I do not sin habitually any longer but freely and gladly love my Lord and my neighbour.

I find Methodist spirituality to be vital and dynamic, personal and corporate, practical and prayerful, biblical and full of the grace of God.

THE ANGLICAN WAY

In the second place, *Anglicanism* as it is expressed through the traditional Prayer-Book spirituality: that is, through the methodical use of the Book of Common Prayer as the basis for Sunday worship and daily devotions. Again I use the first person singular.

Having been baptised as an infant I was prepared by my vicar for Confirmation by the Bishop when I was a teenager. I had to learn the Catechism (in the Book of Common Prayer) and this gave me much insight into what is the Church, a sacrament, the apostles' creed, the ten commandments and my duty towards God and my neighbour. Of my duty to God I learned that:

> My duty towards God is to believe in him, to fear him, and to love him with all my heart, with all my mind, with all my soul and with all my strength; to worship him, to give him thanks, to put my whole trust in him, to call upon him, to honour his holy Name and his Word, and to serve him truly all the days of my life.

and of my duty to my fellow human beings I learned that:

> My duty towards my neighbour is to love him as myself and to do to all men as I would they should do unto me: to love, honour and succour my father and mother, to honour and obey the King/Queen and all that are put in authority under him/her; to submit myself to all my governors, teachers, spiritual pastors and masters: to order myself lowly and reverently to all my betters: to hurt nobody by word or deed; to be true and just in all my dealing; to bear no malice nor

hatred in my heart; to keep my hands from picking and stealing, and my tongue from evil-speaking, lying and slandering: to keep my body in temperance, soberness and chastity: not to covet nor desire other men's goods; but to learn and labour truly to get mine own living, and to do my duty in that state of life, unto which it shall please God to call me.

It took some time for all this to become true and felt duty for me, as I attended public worship each Sunday and read several devotional books recommended to me by my priest.

Then I began to use the service of Morning Prayer as the basis for my own prayers each morning. I honestly confessed my sins to God, carefully read the appointed lessons from Holy Scripture and meditated on a part of one of them (or from the appointed psalms). And I used the collects (set prayers) to summarise the various petitions and intercessions that I had in my own heart for myself and people around me. By this method I gradually found myself growing in appreciation of the contents of the Bible, of the basic doctrine of the Creed, of the path of prayer, and of the implications for Christian living. Further, the Church Year took on a growing significance and, to my surprise, I even found that my soul was ready to engage in the self-examination and fasting associated with the right keeping of Lent. Also I discovered a deep reverence and love of God in my heart.

Later, without letting go of the morning discipline of 'The Order of Morning Prayer', I also used, as often as I could, 'The Order of Evening Prayer'. Further, I resolved to receive Holy Communion not only each Lord's Day but also on festival days (for example, Ascension Day) and Saints' Days (for example, St Peter's Day). Doing this I find that my love of the Lord Jesus increases as I seek to come to the holy table in true faith to receive his sacramental body and blood.

Through the use of the old Prayer Book in a disciplined way I believe that I am drawing near to God – as he has drawn near to me in the Lord Jesus Christ through the Holy Spirit. Further, I believe that I gain the resolution and strength and wisdom to seek to do each day my duties towards my God and my neighbour. I am finding that the Prayer Book is a kind of instrument and channel used by the Holy Spirit to help me respond to God in a balanced and committed way, ever open to new experiences of his grace and power.

Further, I am finding that my increasing use of the set services of the Prayer Book (i.e. the use of Liturgy) helps me to recognise and be a participant in three liturgies – through the Spirit in the liturgy of heaven where the redeemed and angels together sing, 'To him . . . be praise and honour and glory and power for ever and ever' (Rev 5:13); in the liturgy of the people of God here and now 'With angels and archangels and all the company of heaven we laud and magnify thy glorious name'; and in the liturgy of the heart each day 'My heart and soul praise Thee, O Lord'.

THE CHARISMATIC WAY

Finally, we look at the spirituality of the *pentecostal/charismatic* movement. Here I shall not use the first person singular but rather offer a description as an onlooker. Here we are to think of a twentieth-century movement in two phases. First of all, at the beginning of the century there was a revivalist movement which led to the formation of what are called Pentecostal denominations – for example the Elim and Assemblies of God Churches. Its distinctive characteristic was the claim that after being converted to God there was need for all believers to have a second experience of the grace of God – the being baptised in/by the Holy Spirit, followed by the speaking in tongues (as happened on the Day of Pentecost as described in Acts 2).

In the second place, since World War II there has been a 'renewal' movement within the older denominations, including the Roman Catholic. Here the distinctive characteristic has been the insistence that the supernatural gifts of the Spirit (1 Cor 12:8–10) are available to the Church today through the sovereign distribution of the exalted Lord Jesus Christ. The Greek for gifts is *charisma* and thus the expression 'charismatic movement'. Further, like the older Pentecostalism, this movement has insisted that every believer ought to be baptised in/by/with the Holy Spirit either at conversion or at a later time in order to experience to the full the presence and power of the Lord Jesus. Thus apart from believing that the Son of God became man to provide salvation for us the charismatic believes that he is very active now in his world, working in and through the Holy Spirit, and the effects of his presence are to be expected, felt and seen in signs and wonders, changed lives, free 'spiritual' worship, and great joy.

Therefore the contribution of the charismatic movement to people within traditional denominations has been to make them appreciate in a deeper and more vital way the basic teaching and practice they have long known. For Protestant evangelicals the Word of God is both He who and that which is brought to life in a contemporary encounter through the agency of the Holy Spirit – the Spirit of Christ who inspired the writers of Scripture. For Roman Catholics the sacrament of the body and blood of Christ (Eucharist/Mass) is not only that which is the major service of the Church but also a personal encounter with the living Lord Jesus who presides at the Eucharist and freely gives himself to those who eat the bread and drink the sacramental wine.

Apart from giving new vitality, meaning and purpose to the traditional forms of worship, charismatic spirituality has certain distinctive expressions which are to be found whether it be inside the Roman Catholic or a major Protestant Church. Here are several of them, which follow on from the primary experience of being baptised in/with/by the Holy Spirit.

(a) *Freedom in worship*. Not only is worship seen as of central importance in the Christian life, but it is more active and physical – tapping of feet, clapping of hands, raising of arms, and dancing before the Lord. Such worship may be additional to the traditional services or part of them. Further, there is in use a great variety of songs (see, for example, the songbooks, *Living Waters* and *Songs of Fellowship*) which are mostly corporate rather than individual expressions of praise and prayer.

(b) *Spiritual gifts in worship and personal prayer*. Alongside

the freedom in the physical realm, there is the exercise of the
supernatural gifts of the Spirit. One will speak in tongues,
another will interpret; and yet another will prophesy. Then
perhaps others will lay their hands upon a sick brother/sister
and pray for healing, inner and physical.

In private prayer the charismatic Christian will exercise the
gift of speaking in tongues by praying in the Spirit and even
singing in the Spirit to the Lord.

Further, there is an emphasis upon every member ministry
because of the belief that God has given to all at least one
supernatural gift of the Spirit (as well as sanctifying and direct-
ing natural gifts). Thus there is less emphasis upon the
'ordained' ministry and more emphasis upon the ministry of
each and every person than in traditional western Christianity.

(c) *Living in community*. With the increase in corporate thinking by charismatics, there have appeared a growing number of
communities – small and large – bound by simple rules and
seeking to live together to express true Christian family living.
They are often 'covenant communities' where members
covenant with each other to help one another and as a group
to serve the neighbourhood. This means that participants enjoy
both personal, private prayer along with community prayer and
celebration each day.

So we see that for the individual charismatic there is the possibility that the basic aim/goal of spirituality and ways/means
towards it as taught in her/his denomination can be given an
extra dimension of depth and vitality through the experience
of the renewing presence and power of the Spirit of Christ. Or
there is the possibility of creating a spirituality which is only
that of the emphases within this renewal movement. The
former would seem to be preferable.

Recognising that there are several valid expressions of spirituality for a Christian today, what am I to do? The fact is that
God calls me to holiness and righteousness as a member of a
specific local church, where I belong. I need to discover the
depth and width of the tradition of prayer and praise, medi-

tation and contemplation, discipline and consecration from which my church is fed. It may be a wide tradition (as say in a parish of the Church of England) or a more concentrated tradition (as say in a House or Calvinistic Baptist church). I must see which aspects of the tradition of spirituality speak/appeal/minister to me now and make full use of them, recognising that others will seem to be 'for me' later. Also I must realise how God is ready to minister to me through my fellow members as well as through others with whom my church has fraternal relations. In other words, before I go off in search of something else (more exciting? more palatable?) I need to exhaust God's supply through my own tradition (and I shall probably find that it is a rich supply!).

16

Variety in Personality

God calls everyone to perfection, holiness and righteousness; but no two of us are alike – similar perhaps in many ways but not the same. Each of us has her/his own personality; further, individual, personal circumstances vary from person to person. We may say that some differences between us are ordained by God (for example, racial types), and some are the result of a variety of historical, economic and social factors (for example, some live in fine houses in a good environment while others exist in slums).

Though we speak the same language, watch the same television programmes, buy the same packaged foods, wear the same ready-made clothing, use the same electrical, electronic and mechanical equipment, and drive the same basic types of car, we are not thereby changed into a vast army of identical persons. It is true that people tend to do what the crowd does; but, each of us remains herself/himself. However much I eat, drink, and live as others do, I remain myself.

SIMILAR BUT NOT IDENTICAL

Take the matter of human personality. We know from observation and experience that there are various types of personality – for example, the shy and retiring, and the extrovert and ebullient. Further, we know that while an individual may be slotted into one or another of the basic personality types described by psychologists she/he is not thereby identical with others who are placed in that type. For there is variety within and across types and each individual is unique, having a personality which is only hers/his.

Further, we recognise that personality is psychosomatic – it is, we may say, the outward reflection of the total person, body and soul. In fact the general shape or structure of personality is fixed by heredity and therefore it has to be accepted as part of God's creation. However, that shape or structure is moulded by the total environment in which a child is reared and educated. Thus home, school, and general culture all affect the development of personality and temperament.

Therefore, when I am converted to Jesus Christ (be it as a teenager or later in life) and decide to take Christian spirituality seriously I have to accept who I am and from where I must begin. My personality, of whatever kind it is, is mine and cannot be swopped for another – this I must accept, as I also must accept God's gracious forgiveness of all my sins. But I must accept myself, my personality, in the knowledge that the Spirit of the Lord Jesus desires to renovate, renew and redirect it so that it becomes the vehicle for holiness and joy, love and righteousness.

As I respond to the grace of God my character will be changed from that of self-seeking to that of God-seeking and from that of self-love to that of love for the neighbour. Yet it will be I, with my particular personality, whose character is being changed. And because it is a different personality from that of fellow Christians, the way I respond to God will be similar but not identical with their response. They may find one form of meditation helpful while I may use another: they may prefer liturgical worship while I may prefer a more free type of worship: they may find the example of St Francis of Assisi a great encouragement while I may find that of William Carey more challenging; and they may find it possible to take alcoholic beverages while I feel I must never drink them.

Variety in personality requires variety in forms and aspects of Christian spirituality. Pastors and spiritual directors need to bear this in mind when advising people: and each of us must recognise that what is good for another is not necessarily good for oneself. There are many acceptable ways of responding to God in faith, obedience and love.

VARIED CONTEXTS

Not only have we different personalities we also have different personal circumstances. And the latter also affect the type of spirituality we adopt. Some circumstances can, of course, be changed (though that is easier said than done). I can change my house – if there is another to occupy and buy; I can change my job – if another employer will offer me work; I can change my car – if I can afford to buy another. But I cannot change the fact that I am a mother or father, son or daughter, brother or sister.

I must accept that God has placed me in particular circumstances and relationships, which he may not want me to attempt to change. It is my duty to respond to his call to be holy within these circumstances, not despite them. And the form of spirituality I choose, adopt and develop must take into account my real situation. This context must not conquer me but I must master it for the sake of Jesus, my Lord.

Take, for example, Christians in the following circumstances:

1. A retired lady, living alone, in good health and with adequate finances. She is free to develop a spirituality which includes much participation in corporate worship, retreats, works of mercy and fellowship. And this form may be the best for her.

2. A young mother with two children under five. Her husband is out from morning until evening at least five days a week and she is left at home. She finds it difficult to make space and time for daily meditation and prayer and when the children are asleep she is too tired to pray. She has to learn from other women who have been through her experiences what are the options and how she can keep intact her communion with the Lord.

3. A businessman whose work takes him regularly far from home and family. He is often staying in hotels and has a good expense account to cover food, drink and entertainment. The temptations he faces can be quite powerful and thus as a priority he has to make space and time each day for his meditation and prayer in order to keep his vision clear and his

commitment to Jesus firm. How he actually goes about meditating and praying will depend to a great extent (as we have noted) on his personality and temperament.

4. A student is away from home at college/university and finding a freedom never previously experienced. Freedom requires responsibility to use it aright. She/he will need to be much in prayer and often in Christian fellowship in order to have the determination and strength to walk with the Lord Jesus in the way of holiness. It is so easy to go with the crowd and thereby to fall away from the following of Jesus.

Examples could be multiplied. However, there are various principles to be borne in mind. One is that my daily duty to meditate/pray/worship is not instead of my duty within a family, in my employment and in service of my neighbour (hood). It is beneath, alongside and through these duties. Another is that I ought to accept my circumstances on the understanding that 'we know that in all things God works for the good of those who love him, who have been called according to his purpose' (Rom 8:28). Thus, for example, making myself unsettled by thinking of other places I could be and other things I could do is working contrary to God's grace. And yet a further principle is that the priority which I must give to worship/prayer in my life (for I am God's child and must keep in touch with him) is in essence and first of all offered in the heart and mind before it becomes a particular activity in a certain place and at a given time. Thus if I cannot find the place and make the time (for example, my children will not leave me in peace) then I can still worship the Lord in my heart. And I can utter a prayer over and over again such as the Lord's Prayer or what is called the Jesus Prayer – 'Lord Jesus Christ, Son of God, have mercy upon me, a sinner'.

In other words, spirituality is not merely and only the cultivation of good ideas and feelings in the soul: it is the whole person responding to God's grace and call with a particular personality and within specific circumstances. And wherever I am, be it in the inner city or isolated countryside, in a Christian community house or a student's hostel, the call to be perfect, holy and righteous becomes constant.

PSYCHOSPIRITUAL MATURITY

God calls each of us wherever we are and whatever our vocation to both psychological and spiritual maturity. In fact there cannot be one without the other for it is clear (if we reflect on the matter) that we relate to God through the same structure and mechanisms of personality as we actually relate to fellow human beings. This means, for example, the maturity of the teenager will be that appropriate to her/his stage of human and spiritual development. We recall that our Lord Jesus did not begin his public ministry until he was around thirty years of age, and had by that time achieved both psychological as well as spiritual maturity (see Luke 2:52).

Much of this book has been about spiritual and moral maturity and so what is needed here is an account of psychological maturity. For this we turn to Adrian van Kaam who writes:

A mature person is one who has begun to care for the wholeness of his life. He tries to grow beyond the volatility of childish sentiment and youthful excitements. His life becomes less impulsive or compulsive. He begins to live by wise reflections, by basic inner conviction and lasting commitment. He accepts responsibility for the life direction he has discovered to be his, no matter how pedestrian and prosaic this life may seem to others. He is no longer obsessed by the extraordinary and the spectacular. His need to be noticed, to be popular and liked is diminished. He grows in generous solidarity with others in society and community. He accepts and copes wisely with the sufferings and limitations everyday life imposes on all human beings. He is at home with his own failures, limits and imperfections. Without excessive guilt feelings he tries to make the best of his life in a relaxed and gentle way. No longer does he drift off in dreams, idle fantasies, floating idealism. He forbids himself the debilitating pleasures of playing fantasy games with the harsh reality of today and tomorrow. He probes the facts and tries to improve the human situation a little every day, leaving the rest in the hands of God. ('Am I on the road to psychological and spiritual maturity?', National Catholic News Service Series, 1979)

When such maturity is fused with the growth towards spiritual maturity then of course the latter sets the tone of the psychological maturity. For true psychological maturity from a Christian perspective can only be reached when the whole person is totally and lovingly submitted to the Lord Jesus – in thoughts, feelings, intentions, and actions. All aspects of the personality need to be orientated towards God who becomes the integrating focus of all maturity. In fact Christ is both the Goal and the Energiser of the growth to maturity.

In his very helpful *Psychotherapy and the Spiritual Quest* (1988), David Benner speaks of psychospiritual maturity. This involves maturity of both the basic psychological and spiritual aspects of personality. The psychological (or as he calls it the structural) development is through five stages (from the symbiotic dependency of the infant on the mother, through differentiation of self, relatedness, individuation, self-transcendence to the integration of personality): he calls these structural milestones. The maturity or wholeness, he explains, 'is not to be found apart from meaningful engagement with others, significant integration of conscious and unconscious aspects of personality, and a self-transcendence that involves surrender to and service of a larger cause or being' (p.130).

The spiritual or directional milestones are based on what Protestant theologians have called the *ordo salutis* (the order of salvation – that is how experienced by the repentant, believing sinner). He lists eight milestones – development of basic trust; awareness of call to self-transcendence; recognition of call as from God; awareness of insufficiency of self (sinfulness); receipt of divine forgiveness; progressive freedom from sin; progressive evidence of the fruit of the Spirit and deepening intimacy with God.

Dr Benner insists that the model should not be interpreted as being strictly linear for the stages in each sphere of functioning are not absolutely fixed. The real message of this model is that growth in the two spheres is interdependent. Problems of one sphere become also problems for the other. And spiritual growth requires at least a certain degree of psychological maturity. Thus, in some cases, psychotherapy can actually help some people to grow spiritually because it helps them towards psychological maturity and thereby releases in them the possibility (led by the Spirit) of growth in holiness.

In summarising his model of psychospirituality Dr Benner writes: 'Psychospiritual maturity is characterized by integration of personality, which occurs within a context of significant interpersonal relationships and surrender to God. In this surrender we discover our true selves. The integrated self, which is the endpoint of this process, is both an achievement and a gift. In intimate union with God we find the selves he gives us: we become the selves we are intended to be from eternity' (p.133).

God has made us all in his image and after his likeness: but we are all different. When we reach spiritual and psychological maturity we remain different and through the variety of personalities the creative work of God in nature and in grace is reflected.

17

For me if . . .

When my context and personality-type have been analysed, I remain. I exist as myself. But I do not remain alone or in isolation. The Lord God, my Creator and my Saviour, is always with me: I cannot escape from him even if I wish to do so. He loves me with an everlasting love and he persistently and graciously invites me to walk in his way and be his friend. He calls me to be the kind of trusting, loving, obedient creature he intended should exist when he made the human race. And he offers me every help to be such a person.

Yet I know that to respond to his call is not like responding to an invitation to join a society which will take only a small part of my time, energy and money. It is to answer the call of the Creator and Judge of the whole universe, the almighty God, who is all-knowing and utterly pure in essence and righteous in all his ways.

So, as a mere creature addressed by her/his Creator, I must take time to consider the call of God and carefully reflect upon what he both promises and demands of me. I need to allow the full force of who it is who speaks to me to be impressed upon my heart and mind: I need to be truly aware of what in real terms the situation in which I find myself truly is. Perhaps I ought to ask myself the following questions.

1. *Do I wish – indeed ought I – to embrace as the primary aim of my life the call of God to be perfect, holy and righteous, in the imitation of Jesus?* To say 'yes' is to reject all the possible primary aims in life which contemporary western society - explicitly or implicitly – commends. These include financial and personal success in business and profession, owning a fine home

filled with attractive furniture and every modern convenience, owning two cars, taking several overseas holidays each year, being a member of the 'right' clubs or societies and so on. In the words of Jesus it is to say 'yes' to seeking first the kingdom of God and his righteousness, in the knowledge that God will supply all our needs according to his grace in Jesus Christ.

Because I put the imitation of the Lord Jesus first does not mean that I shall fail in business, or live in a hovel, or have no friends in business, or engage in leisure activities. God can make the one who seeks after his righteousness to have plenty of this world's success and riches: yet such a person can never love these and prize them. For in his heart he knows that the love of riches is not only the root of evil but also it is so much inferior to the love of God, the supreme excellence and beauty. Success and riches are to be used to serve the kingdom of God.

I need to be fully aware that to be committed to the imitation of Jesus in his character and virtues is to be committed to that which the world will generally regard as either odd or mad, stupid or weird! Indeed, the world may well exert all kinds of pressure on me to make me conform to one or another of its standards and these pressures may be a kind of persecution. Thus to be called to perfection and holiness may mean to be involved in suffering with and for Jesus Christ: to be called to righteousness and godliness may mean to be involved in deprivation both of goods and reputation.

But am I prepared for the commitment of spending much time with my God in meditation and prayer to get to know him, to admire him, to love him, to worship him and to see his virtues and graces (that I may imitate him)? Do I realise that I shall have to give a high priority to seeking the Lord in private each and every day?

2. *Do I wish – ought I desire – to be filled with the Spirit of Christ?* The world in which I live pressurises me to fill my soul with all kinds of substitutes for the living God, who made me in order to place his Spirit within me. Ambition, pride of place or position, doubts and fears, self-fulfilment, self-satisfaction, sexual passions and the good feelings created by drugs are all out there competing for the centre of my soul.

Only as I am continually filled with the Spirit who indwelt and rested upon the Lord Jesus can I be the person whom God created me to be. Only by his presence in my heart and mind can I know who I really am – a child of God, loved by him and destined by him to be truly fulfilled in his service both in this age and the age to come. Only by his Spirit can I resist those powerful forces that would take me over to make me their servant and slave. For I am not a whole person; I am not really myself; I am not truly and wholly human unless the Spirit of my Creator/Saviour is present in and with me. I am made in the image, after the likeness, of my God and I can only function as such if the Spirit of the Lord Jesus is there to cause my soul to reflect the divine virtues.

Am I prepared to put myself in the position where I can truly be continually filled with the Spirit of the Lord? Am I willing to wait upon the Lord so that my soul can become a reservoir and channel which he can always fill with his loving Spirit?

3. *Am I ready – ought I – to embrace the necessary commitment, discipline, consecration and self-mortification involved in authentic Christian spirituality?* I recall that Jesus had much to say about the readiness to be wholehearted and single-minded in commitment and loyalty to the kingdom of God. You cannot serve two masters and you cannot go in two directions at the same time! To choose to be with Jesus on God's side is to choose to oppose sin, evil, and the devil, as these appear both around me and in me.

I do not know what God will send to me or allow to happen to me: all I know is that he loves me with an everlasting and infinite love and I cannot fail to reach his Goal if I look to him and trust him. However, I am aware that if I am to trust God wholeheartedly there is much in my soul which will have to be put to death or cast out – my pride, self-sufficiency, self-justification and self-satisfaction. In fact I do not really know what God will want me to abandon, give up, mortify or exclude for his sake and my true good! Yet I know that anything I give up will be like losing a penny to gain a massive fortune, if in giving up selfishness I gain the glory of God. But to say this, and to set off on a course which will involve putting it to the test, are two different things! Am I willing to set course for the annihilation of my sinful self and the receiving of the presence of the living Christ to create a new self?

4. *Do I desire – ought I to want to desire – to be with Jesus, the Lord, and to share his love and glory for ever?* This is a strange – even an odd – question! Living in such an affluent society and in such a beautiful world (despite the effects of pollution) why should I want to be elsewhere? But let me think about it more.

Where does a lover want to be? With her/his beloved. Anyone who is a genuine disciple of Jesus and knows the partial joy of his presence (via the Holy Spirit) will surely want to be with him in a more engaging and fulfilling way – face to face. To love Jesus Christ as Lord and Saviour and to believe that to serve him is the greatest privilege of all is surely to want to be as near to him as it is possible to be. And that means to be with him where he is. Is such a desire in my heart? Would it thrill me beyond words to be lifted instantaneously into his presence?

Of course I realise that he may want me to stay on earth for a long time to serve him in the vocation he has given me. And if he does then I ought to be willing and ready to serve him fully and faithfully every new day. Yet, at the same time, if I do not also each day heartily desire to be with him and to know the power of his love more intensely, then I cannot see how I can really serve him adequately day by day. In fact I suspect – indeed I believe I know – that in proportion as I desire to be with him in glory so shall I faithfully and lovingly serve him in my vocation here.

5. *Do I wish – indeed ought I – to give myself wholeheartedly and unreservedly in the serving of others?* To say 'yes' is to be prepared to serve the deprived, poor, awkward, dirty, smelly and depraved as readily and extensively as the nice, acceptable, decent, appreciative and responsible. It is to be no respecter of persons in the giving of love, time and commitment. It is to do everything gladly for Christ's sake, expecting no reward or

even thanks. The life of service is to give, as a true disciple of Jesus, love where there is hatred, pardon where there is injury, hope where there is despair, joy where there is sadness and light in all darkness. It is to give and not count the cost, to fight and not heed the wounds, to toil and seek no rest, to labour and not ask for any reward, except that of knowing that God's will is being done.

Am I prepared for a way of life from which all concern for self-fulfilment and self-justification must be removed? For I cannot truly serve others freely and gladly if I am thinking of my own needs and ambitions.

Further, this life of serving others for Jesus' sake will have to be done primarily through the vocation that God has given to me. This means in the family as a father or mother, a brother or sister, cousin or uncle: and also in the church as a member of the family of God and household of faith, loving my fellow members in practical services and ways. But while 'charity begins at home' it does not end there. People whom I meet in the work that God has given me – be it in the office, classroom, factory or subway ticket-office – are those from whom God may be choosing some to be the recipients of his grace through me. So I am not only to do what I have to do in my work as unto the Lord – as if I were doing it directly for him: I also have to treat people whom I meet as he treated people wherever he met them – as the One who came to serve.

If you wish to intensify the probing of your soul and its inner desires/motivations, you could go on and engage in such exercises as the following:

a. Read through the Beatitudes in Matthew 5:1–11, consider carefully what type of character they describe, and then ask yourself if this is what you want to be like. (You could do the same exercise also for 1 Corinthians 13.)

b. Read very carefully through the descriptions Paul gives of what serving the Lord Jesus and the church of God meant in real terms for him in the Roman Empire (2 Cor 4:8–11; 6:4–10); and ask yourself whether or not you are prepared for such service and suffering?

c. Read one or more of the best poems/hymns which speak of
utter and ready dedication to the Lord Jesus and ask yourself
if you are prepared to make such commitment. Here is one by
Bishop T. Ken (1637–1711) originally written for boys to use
each morning at Winchester College:

1   Awake my soul, and with the sun
Thy daily stage of duty run;
Shake off dull sloth, and joyful rise
To pay thy morning sacrifice

2   Redeem thy mis-spent time that's past
Live this day as if 'twere thy last:
Improve thy talent with due care;
For the great Day thyself prepare.

3   Let all thy converse be sincere,
Thy conscience as the noon-day clear;
Think how all-seeing God thy ways
And all thy secret thoughts surveys.

4   By influence of the light Divine
Let thy own light in good works shine;
Reflect all heaven's propitious ways
In ardent love and cheerful praise.

Part 2

5   Wake, and lift up thyself, my heart,
And with the Angels bear thy part,
Who all night long unwearied sing
High praise to the eternal King.

6   Awake, awake, ye heavenly choir,
May your devotion me inspire,
That I like you my age may spend,
Like you may on my God attend.

Part 3

7   Glory to thee, who safe has kept
And hast refreshed me whilst I slept;

Grant, Lord, when I from death shall wake
I may of endless light partake.

8   Heaven is, dear Lord, where'er thou art,
O never then from me depart;
For to my soul 'tis hell to be
But for one moment void of thee.

9   Lord, I my vows to thee renew;
Scatter my sins as morning dew;
Guard my first springs of thought and will,
And with thyself my spirit fill.

10   Direct, control, suggest, this day
All I design, or do, or say;
That all my powers, with all their might,
In thy sole glory may unite.

11   Praise God, from whom all blessings flow,
Praise him, all creatures here below,
Praise him above, ye heavenly host,
Praise Father, Son, and Holy Ghost. Amen.

Other hymns you could use could include 'Forth in thy name,
O Lord, I go' by Charles Wesley, 'O Jesus I have promised'
by John E. Bode, and 'Fill thou my life, O Lord my God' by
Horatius Bonar.

Soul searching in the presence of the Lord Jesus Christ is very
demanding. However, the eyes that behold you are filled with
love and encouragement. The pain of letting go all that hinders
the receiving of his love will soon be forgotten in the joy of
experiencing that same love.

18

A Personal Covenant

The time has come for a decision to be made – or heartily confirmed. You will surely have decided that you want both to stand with Jesus and to walk in and with him in the path of holiness and righteousness, service and ministry.

What I urge you to do is to make a solemn covenant with the Lord, your God – or, rather bind yourself to the covenant which he in Christ Jesus has made with you. The initiative has already been taken: I urge you to respond with all your soul.

To do this you need to allow space and time in order to make it a memorable occasion. You must not be rushed but be able to think and pray calmly and reverently in a quiet place where you will not be disturbed. I suggest that you proceed in this manner:

1. Commit the place and time to God, asking him to bless you as you come before him. And recall that he is with you in this very place at this specific time.

2. Read Joshua 24 and meditate upon verses 21–22, 'We will serve the Lord'.

3. Read Hebrews 8 and 10:11–25 and meditate upon 10:22, 'Let us draw near with a true heart in full assurance of faith . . .'

4. Recall the great facts of the gospel of God concerning Jesus – that God loves us, Christ suffered and died for us, that Christ rose from the dead and was exalted in heaven for us, that he sent the Holy Spirit to us to act on his behalf, that he will come again to judge the living and the dead, and that there

will be a new age in the kingdom of God in which the righteous will dwell everlastingly.

Persuade your soul that God offers you his full salvation in Jesus through the Holy Spirit.

5. Make your response by a solemn covenant. (I advise you to write it out so that you can recall it monthly or annually or whenever the occasion or need arises.)

The following may serve as a guide to the kind of covenant and engagement you will make. Do not repeat it verbatim but adapt it to your own needs or reject it in favour of one you write wholly by yourself. You may feel the need for a shorter or a longer form of commitment. And, from time to time, you may feel guided by the Holy Spirit to amend your covenant in the direction of an even more explicit consecration of your whole self – body, mind and spirit – to the Lord Jesus.

A Suggested Covenant with the Lord

O eternal and ever-blessed God. I desire to present myself before you. I fully recognise that I have been, and remain to this day, your sinful and disobedient creature. There is no merit in me which brings me into your holy presence. Indeed, who am I that I dare come before the King of all kings in order to make a covenant with him? I am a mere mortal but I declare that the covenant I come to make is really yours and the invitation to make it is also yours. You have offered it to me in and through your Son: and you have inclined my heart gratefully to accept it.

So I come as did the tax-collector who would only cry out, 'God be merciful to me, a sinner'. I come pleading nothing but the sacrificial blood of Jesus and his perfect righteousness. For his sake I ask that you be merciful to me, now and always, O Lord God, sinner that I am. For I am convinced of your absolute right to own me and I desire nothing so much as that you will claim me and make me wholly your own. Make me, I pray, a worthy partner in your covenant of grace.

Today, the . . . . . . day of . . . . . . in the year . . . . . . being in a solemn and serious mood, I surrender myself to you.

I renounce all former lords and powers who have had dominion over me. I reject Satan, evil and sin, and I consecrate all that I am and all that I have to you. I desire that I be used entirely for your glory and resolutely employed in obedience to your commands, as long as you give me life here on earth. And I determine to hold myself always in an attentive posture to observe the first intimations of your will, and to be ready to spring forward, with zeal and joy, to the immediate execution of it.

I leave, O Lord, to your management and direction all I possess and all I wish; and I set every enjoyment and every interest before you to be disposed of as you please. Continue or remove what you have given to me; bestow or refuse what I imagine I want as you, O Lord, shall see good. And though I dare not say I will never complain; yet I truly hope I may venture to say that I will endeavour not only to submit but to acquiesce; not only to bear whatever you send or place upon me but also to consent to it and praise you for it; and always contentedly fusing my will with yours looking upon myself as nothing and upon you, O Lord, as the great eternal All.

I resolve, O my God, to be a faithful member of your Church, loving my brothers and sisters in Christ, serving them in whatever ways are appropriate for your kingdom, and submitting myself to their ministry, advice and direction. I want all my human relationships to be sweetened by the love of Jesus.

Use me, O Lord, I beseech you as an instrument for your glory and in your service. May I, through doing and suffering what you shall appoint, bring some revenue of praise to you and be of benefit to the world in which I dwell. Let me be sanctified by your Spirit. Transform me more and more into the image of your Son. Impart to me through him all the needful influence of your purifying and comforting Spirit. And let my life be spent under these influences and in the light of your gracious favour, as my Father and my God.

Dispose my affairs, O my God, in a manner which may be most subservient to your glory and my own true and genuine happiness. And when I have done and borne your will on earth, call me, I pray, at what time and in what way you please into life beyond mortal death.

When the solemn hour of death comes may I remember this covenant – as I know you will remember it, O God, for Jesus Christ's sake. Embrace me at that sacred moment in your everlasting arms. Put strength and confidence into my departing spirit. And receive it into the abode of all those who rest in Jesus, peacefully and joyfully to await the accomplishment of your great promise to all your people – even that of a glorious resurrection and of eternal happiness in your heavenly presence.

Glory be to the Father, and to the Son,
    and to the Holy Spirit:
as it was in the beginning, is now,
    and shall be for ever. Amen.

Signed. . . . . .

6. Having solemnly repeated it before God and signed it in his holy presence, it is appropriate to spend time praising the name of the Lord. For this purpose there is nothing better than the psalms of praise (145–50) which end the Psalter.

7. Make a note in your diary to keep an anniversary of the signing of this covenant as a day of praise, prayer and fasting, in order to renew it in God's presence.

8. You may find it helpful to take it with you, say each month, to the celebration of the Lord's Supper (the meal of God's covenant of grace), and there renew your commitment to the Lord's covenant, sealed by his blood.

Epilogue

Since the third century of the Christian era the sisters Martha and Mary have been interpreted as symbols of two different but complementary aspects or dimensions of spirituality. Let us read Luke 10:38–42 and then meditate upon the descriptions given there of the two sisters as they related to Jesus, the Messiah.

> Jesus came to a village where a woman named Martha opened her home to him. She had a sister called Mary, who sat at the Lord's feet listening to what he said. But Martha was distracted by all the preparations that had to be made. She came to him and asked, 'Lord don't you care that my sister has left me to do the work by myself? Tell her to help me!'
>
> 'Martha, Martha,' the Lord answered, 'you are worried and upset about many things, but only one thing is needed. Mary has chosen what is better, and it will not be taken away from her.'

Here to lead you in reflection is my own brief meditation.

A MEDITATION

Lord Jesus, I think I understand Martha. For her your visit to her home was a rare and special occasion. Nothing less than the best would do. The house must be spotless, the table laid with the best crockery, the meal rich and varied, and the service first-class. So she rushed and fussed and cooked. There was much to do and she got herself all hot and bothered: and she felt worse because Mary did not share her passionate concern to make everything to be the very best whatever the cost.

Lord Jesus, I think I appreciate what you were looking for. You were on your way to Jerusalem. As God's Messiah, called to fulfil the ministry of the Suffering Servant (Is 52–53) you knew you had to go up to Jerusalem and face the authorities there: you expected to be misunderstood, maltreated and executed. There was much on your mind and much in your heart. You did not want special food or an over-tidy house. You desired a peaceful home, friendly appreciation, loving understanding and simple sustenance. You looked for an oasis of calm where you could relax amongst sympathetic friends.

Lord Jesus, I think I understand Mary. She realised that you were an extraordinary Rabbi, a very special teacher and master. She knew that you had much to say and do for the Lord God, the God of Abraham, Isaac and Jacob. She felt that great matters weighed upon your mind and heart and you wanted rest, peace and quiet. And if you cared to talk then she wanted to be on hand to catch every word and treasure it. So she decided that the best way to serve you was to sit at your feet, ready both to hear you and to do your bidding.

Lord Jesus, I think I appreciate what you said to Martha. I must first of all, though, confess that I initially thought that you were rather rough with her when you said, 'Mary has chosen what is better . . .'. However, I now see that you did not want a sumptuous spread but a simple meal, not a lot of feverish activity but quiet sympathy and service, and not a spotless home, but attentive hearts. You wanted love expressed according to your need and position (which Mary recognised) not according to Martha's sincere but ill-conceived view. You did not want one sister complaining about the other but two sisters truly waiting upon you as their Master.

Lord Jesus, I appreciate the symbolic truth expressed by each of the sisters. Martha is so obviously the symbol of activity –

getting up and getting on with it. She represents the effort to love God in action. In contrast, Mary is the symbol of loving attention – meditation, prayer, contemplation, worship, loving God with heart, soul and mind.

Further, I can see why the symbol of Mary has always been taken as having a priority over that of Martha (Mary having chosen the better role). Before we engage in serving you we need to find out how you need to be served: we must sit at your feet before we can go off to do what you command. We must hear from you before we can speak for you.

Lord Jesus, help me to get my priority right. We live in a busy world where success implies always being active and mobile. In fact there is a tendency to make activity an end in itself and thus to see time spent in contemplation of your glory as a pleasant but unnecessary diversion. Help me, I pray, to get the balance right, to learn to contemplate you and hear from you before dashing off to do what I think you want to be done. I need to learn of you and from you, for you are my Example and Saviour and Master. If in the guidance of your Spirit I imitate you then I shall happily combine the contemplative and active dimensions of spirituality. Help me to do so, I pray. Amen.

Appendix 1

The Literature of Christian Spirituality

Spirituality is all about living in Christ to the glory of God. The literature generated by this response to God's call to perfection, holiness and righteousness may be usefully divided into three basic kinds.

1. *Instruction and Exhortation*. The most famous books include *The Imitation of Christ* by Thomas à Kempis, *Introduction to the Devout Life* by Francis de Sales and William Law's *A Serious Call to a Devout and Holy Life*. To these can be added many hundreds more. My own contribution to this area is to edit the *Guidebook to the Spiritual Life* (1988) and write *Meditating upon God's Word* (1988). Great care is needed in using modern books for they often combine what may be called 'Eastern' methods with Christian insights and, thereby, sometimes remove themselves from the stream of basic Christian orthodoxy.

2. *Records of Christian experiences of and the response to the grace of our Lord Jesus Christ*. These can either be biographical or autobiographical; also they can take the form of journals or diaries. The most famous book in this category is the *Confessions* of Augustine. From the pen of a lady perhaps the most widely read is the *Life* by Teresa of Avila. Others that are much treasured include the *Journals* of the two Wesley brothers, John and Charles, and of their contemporary, George Whitfield, as well as the *Grace abounding to the chief of sinners* by John Bunyan (from whom we also have, of course, *Pilgrim's Progress*).

To these can be added hundreds more of varying quality,

both in their content and the style. It is wise to read the 'classics' first.

3. *Scientific/theological studies of spirituality*. From the Protestant side there is *The Religious Affections* by Jonathan Edwards and *Das Gebet* (= *Prayer*) by Friedrich Heiler, to name two well known ones. From the Roman Catholic side there is a much richer supply of studies, the most recent in English by Jordan Aumann on *Spiritual Theology*. The latter points to the important studies of John Arintero, Reginald Garrigou-Lagrange, Auguste Poulain and Adolphe Tanquerey, most of which are available in English translations. To these books need to be added the *Dictionaries* of Spirituality (for example, from G. Wakefield and C. Cary-Elwes) and the *Study of Spirituality* (ed. C. Jones, G. Wainwright and E. Yarnold).

Obviously this type of book is only for the student, pastor and theologically educated laity. It is rarely intended to inspire – merely to provide information and analysis.

Appendix 2

Perfectionism

There is a reluctance within classical Protestantism (Lutheranism, Presbyterianism and Anglicanism) to speak of Christian perfection. This hesitancy has two sources. First, the deep consciousness that as long as we remain in our mortal bodies in this world we can never be free from sin; and, secondly, opposition to the common claim made in the fifteenth and early sixteenth centuries that perfection comes through the taking of the monastic vows of chastity, celibacy and obedience. Both these themes appear in the first great Protestant Confession of Faith, the *Augsburg Confession* (1530), which is primarily the work of Martin Luther.

Article 27 is entitled 'Monastic Vows'. In it we read this about Christian perfection:

> The commands of God and true and proper service of God are obscured when people are told that monks alone are in a state of perfection. For this is Christian perfection: that we fear God honestly with our whole hearts, and yet have sincere confidence, faith and trust that for Christ's sake we have a gracious, merciful God: that we may and should ask and pray God for those things of which we have need, and confidently expect help from him in every affliction connected with our particular calling and station in life; and that meanwhile we do good works for others and diligently attend to our calling. True perfection and right service of God consist of these things and not of medicancy or wearing a black or gray cowl . . .

There are several important themes here. For example, the

emphasis that each is to serve God in her/his calling (as parent, butcher, farmer, peasant, teacher and so on) by doing it as unto the Lord, in a state of justification by faith, is fundamental to the whole Protestant teaching on vocation. To be called by God to be a farmer is as important as being called to be an ordained minister and in each vocation the aim is the same – to serve God faithfully. 'It is perfection for each of us with true faith to obey his own calling'; and 'All men, whatever their calling, ought to seek perfection; that is, growth in the fear of God, in faith, in the love of their neighbour, and similar spiritual virtues'.

From this definition of Christian perfection there developed no particular tradition in Lutheranism of speaking of Christian perfection – and the same is true both of Calvinism (Presbyterianism) and the Church of England in its Protestant expression. It was too open to misunderstanding both from a Catholic and a radical Protestant position. The *Augsburg Confessions* not only condemns Catholic teaching on monastic vows but also Anabaptist (= radical, sectarian Protestantism of the 16th century) on perfectionism. 'Our churches condemn the Anabaptists who deny that those who have once been justified can lose the Holy Spirit, and also those who contend that some may attain such perfection in this life that they cannot sin' (Article 12). Similar teaching on the second point can be found in the Calvinist Confessions of Faith.

What Luther called 'Anabaptist' teaching has often come to the surface in Protestant Christianity since the sixteenth century; for example, it was very common in the popular teaching which accompanied the spread of Christianity westwards in the USA in the nineteenth century – that is in frontier religion. And, of course, it comes in various grades of sophistication.

However, alongside this popular expression of the Christian ideal there is within Protestantism a more firmly and historically grounded doctrine of Christian perfection. This may be traced back to the great medieval theologian, Thomas Aquinas, and his treatise *De Perfectione*. In this he teaches that Christian perfection, to which Christ calls his disciples, is nothing less than the perfect loving of God and the neighbour. He also teaches that the best way to this goal is through taking the monastic vows. The emphasis on perfect love was taken up by the Anglican, William Law, in his book *Treatise on Christian Perfection* (1726) and other publications. These were most carefully read by John and Charles Wesley (along with such other books as *The Imitation of Christ* by Thomas à Kempis) and together they sent forth into Britain and the whole world an evangelical doctrine of Christian Perfection, with strong roots in the medieval, Catholic tradition. Naturally, they abandoned the idea of monastic vows and they also added the significant teaching that the way to Christian Perfection is normally via a second experience of God's grace, when the heart is purified and filled with the love of God.

John's teaching is set out in his *A Plain Account of Christian Perfection* (1777) and Charles' is found in many of his hymns. For example, in the last verse of 'O for a heart to praise my God' we read:

> Thy nature, gracious Lord, impart;
>   Come quickly from above,
> Write Thy new name upon my heart,
>   Thy new best name of love.

It is not absolute perfection and it is not sinlessness. It is a state of no habitual sin and of a positive loving of God and the neighbour without hesitation and with joy. This teaching is still officially that of the Methodist Church and it has been adopted by modern denominations which have sprung from Methodist connexions or roots. Mainline Protestants who reject the Wesleyan doctrine usually do so because they hold that it tends to view sin as a cancer that can be 'cut out' of the heart, whereas, they would argue, sin is more like a poison than is in the very blood and bone-marrow and can only be reduced and neutralised, never removed.

The impact of the charismatic movement has been felt in virtually all denominations. However, it has not added anything significant in terms of the call of Christ to be perfect. This is perhaps because the being baptised in/with/by the Holy Spirit is seen primarily in terms of a baptism and infilling of the Spirit who brings spiritual gifts as well as power to witness for Christ.

The call to perfection and holiness is recognised (especially by charismatics in the mainline Protestant denominations) as being a call to a continuing commitment and consecration and to a gradual growth in the Christian virtues. But this call is given new urgency and relevance by the baptism in/with/by the Spirit.

However, where the charismatic movement has affected groups and denominations who already had an emphasis upon a second work of grace ('the second blessing') then the baptism in/with/by the Spirit has fused with this to be the 'appointed' way of entry both into the exercise of spiritual gifts and the life of perfect love. (For those who wish to delve deeper in this matter I recommend M. J. Dieter, *The Holiness Revival of the Nineteenth Century*, 1980; V. Synan, *The Holiness-Pentecostalist Movement in the United States*, 1971; H. Lindström, *Wesley and Sanctification*, 1946; and B. B. Warfield, *Perfectionism*, 1920.)

As a postscript the reader may be interested in my own resolution of this question of, What is perfection? First of all, it is necessary that we have a right view of sin and see it as affecting every part of our soul (mind, heart, will) and body; further, it affects those parts of the mind and heart of which I am not conscious. So it is hardly like a cancer in one place that can by painful surgery be removed. In the second place, a person who, through the help of the indwelling Spirit, is actually loving God more positively and joyfully and delighting to serve the neighbour in loving action will also continue to know and feel her/his sinfulness – and to feel it more intensely. This is because the Spirit is revealing how deeply ingrained in the human personality is sin: thus 'saints' see themselves as the worst of sinners. However, thirdly, it is possible to reach the state of not habitually sinning (this is taught in 1 John – those who are truly born of God do not commit sin). Yet as the mind is enlarged in spiritual understanding, and the conscience through the illumination of the Spirit becomes more tender, the scope of what is seen as sin will increase and so the habit of not sinning will cover a wider spectrum of thinking, feeling and doing. There is no limit to this enlargement of understanding and resolve.